Music Express

Year 2

LESSON PLANS, RECORDINGS, ACTIVITIES, PHOTOCOPIABLES AND VIDEOCLIPS

Series devised by **Maureen Hanke**

Compiled by **Helen MacGregor**   Illustrated by **Alison Dexter**   Edited by **Sheena Roberts**

A & C Black • London

Contents

First published 2002
Reprinted 2003 (twice), 2005 and 2008
by A&C Black Publishers Ltd
38 Soho Square, London W1D 3HB
© 2002 A&C Black Publishers Ltd
ISBN: 978-0-7136-6227-6

Teaching text © Helen MacGregor 2002
Unit headings, unit summary text, learning objectives and outcomes © Qualifications and Curriculum Authority
CD/Videoclips compilation © 2002 A&C Black
CD compilationⓅ 2002 A&C Black
Edited by Sheena Roberts. Designed by Jocelyn Lucas
Cover illustration © Alex Ayliffe 2002
Inside illustrations © Alison Dexter 2002
Audio CD sound engineering by Stephen Chadwick
Videoclips filmed and edited by Jamie Acton-Bond
CD-ROM post production by Ian Shepherd
at Sound Recording Technology

Printed in Great Britain by Caligraving Ltd, Thetford, Norfolk

This book is produced using paper that is made from wood grown in managed, sustainable forests. It is natural, renewable and recyclable. The logging and manufacturing processes conform to the environmental regulations of the country of origin.

Introduction

About Music Express

Music Express provides teaching activities that are imaginative, inspiring and fun.

It has been written especially for classroom teachers. It is:

- user-friendly;
- well planned;
- fully resourced, and
- no music reading is required.

Using Music Express as a scheme of work

National Curriculum

Music Express fulfils the requirements of the Music National Curriculum of England, of Wales and of Northern Ireland and the 5-14 National Guidelines for Scotland.

Learning with *Music Express*, children will gain a broad and balanced musical education. They will:

- learn about and sing songs from around the world including the British Isles;
- learn about music from different periods and genres;
- enjoy music lessons with a balance of listening, composing, performing and appraising.

A steady progression plan has been built into *Music Express*, both within each book and from one year to the next, ensuring consistent musical development.

Opportunities are identified throughout for evaluating the children's work and monitoring their progress.

The English QCA scheme of work for music

Music Express is based on the structure of the QCA scheme of work. It uses the same unit headings, making it easy to navigate, and provides activities to achieve the learning outcomes stated.

The teaching activities in *Music Express* have been drawn from and inspired by A & C Black's extensive classroom music resources.

The units

There are six units in each book. Below is a list of the units in *Music Express Year 2*, as described by the QCA:

The long and the short of it (Unit 3)
'This unit develops children's ability to discriminate between longer and shorter sounds, and to use them to create interesting sequences of sound.'

Feel the pulse (Unit 4)
'This unit develops children's ability to recognise the difference between pulse and rhythm and to perform with a sense of pulse.'

Taking off (Unit 5)
'This unit develops children's ability to discriminate between higher and lower sounds and to create simple melodic patterns.'

What's the score? (Unit 6)
'This unit develops children's ability to recognise different ways sounds are made and changed and to name, and know how to play, a variety of classroom instruments.'

Rain rain go away (Unit 7)
'This unit develops children's ability to recognise how sounds and instruments can be used expressively and combined to create music in response to a stimulus.'

Sounds interesting (Unit 2)
'This unit develops children's ability to identify different sounds and to change and use sounds expressively in response to a stimulus.'

The lessons

Each unit is divided into six, weekly lessons, which are intended to be taught over a half term.

There are three activities per lesson which may be taught in one longer music lesson, or over three shorter lessons to suit your timetable.

Planning

The CD-ROM

The CD-ROM provides a medium term plan and six, weekly lesson plans for each unit. These may be printed out to go in your planning folder.

Whilst it is not necessary when teaching the activities to have the lesson plan alongside, it contains useful information for preparing your lesson. This includes:

- the learning objectives and outcomes;

- a list of the resources and minimal preparation you will need to do before the lesson;

- a vocabulary section which defines the musical terms appropriate to the lesson;

- a suggestion of ways to provide differentiated support for particular activities;

- a lesson extension - a suggestion for taking the lesson further with individuals or the whole class. (The extension activities are particularly useful when teaching a mixed year-group class as they extend the older and/or more able children.)

The book

The book provides step by step teaching notes for each lesson. These are written to be as easy to follow as possible.

There are photocopiables to supplement many of the activities.

Preparation

Music Express is designed to minimise your preparation time.

Look out for the icons next to the activity headings which indicate things you need to prepare.

Key to icons

 Photocopiable icon: some activities require photocopies or activity cards to be made from a particular photocopiable.

 Black CD icon: these tracks are for the children to listen to during an activity.

 Grey CD icon: these tracks are for your reference.

 Videoclip and picture icons: you will need to have access to a computer for an activity to show videoclips and pictures on the CD-ROM. (You might like to use a computer-compatible projector to show the videoclips and pictures on a screen for the whole class to see more easily.)

Other resources

Classroom percussion

You will need to have a range of classroom percussion instruments available.

Many activities suggest several members of the class playing instruments at the same time. If necessary, pupils could share instruments and take turns to play.

Specific activities recommend the instruments you will need, but you should use the instruments that you have available.

For a class of 30 pupils, aim to have at least the following:

- Tuned percussion

  1 alto xylophone

  1 alto metallophone

  1 set of chime bars

  a selection of beaters

- A range of untuned percussion instruments, eg

  tambours

  drums

  wood blocks

  cabassas

  maracas

- Other interesting soundmakers, eg

    ocean drum

    rainmaker

    whistles

    wind chimes

- Electronic keyboards are a very useful resource and should be included whenever possible.

Instrumental lessons

Whenever appropriate, invite members of the class who are having instrumental lessons to bring their instruments into classroom music lessons.

If you are not sure which notes particular instruments use, ask the child's instrumental teacher.

Recording and evaluating

Recording on cassette or video

Have a cassette recorder and blank audio cassettes available during your music lessons. Recording pupils' work is important for monitoring their progress.

Children enjoy listening to their performances and contributing to the evaluation of their own and their classmates' work.

Many activities include movement as well as music. If you have a video camera available, video the performance. If not, invite members of your class or another class to watch and offer feedback.

Help for teachers

Teaching tips and background information

These are provided throughout next to the activity or activities to which they refer.

Dance and movement

Encourage movement in activities where it is not mentioned - it is an important means of musical learning.

Group work

The activities suggest appropriate group sizes. Be flexible, especially if your class has little or no experience of group work. Group work may be introduced into classroom music lessons gradually. Those activities which suggest group work may also be managed as whole class activities.

Teaching songs

We hope that teachers will lead the singing with their own voice, particularly with younger children. But in all instances we have assumed that the teacher will use the CD.

If you feel confident, teach yourself a song using the CD and then teach it to the children.

To rehearse songs with your class without the CD, you might:

- sing the melody without the words, to lah or dee;
- chant the rhythm of the words;
- sing the song line by line for the children to copy.

Teachers' videoclips

There are seventeen videoclips on the CD-ROM that demonstrate useful teaching techniques to use in class music lessons.

Clip	Contents
T 01	The Music Express Song
T 02	Teaching a song line by line
T 03	Demonstrating pitch with hand
T 04	Starting together: speed and starting note
T 05	Internalising
T 06	Conducting with a score
T 07	Conducting getting louder
T 08	Inventing vocal ostinatos
T 09	Dividing a class into groups
T 10	Conducting start and stop
T 11	Building layers of sound
T 12	Playing a drone accompaniment
T 13	Recognising a word rhythm
T 14	Allocating accompaniment instruments
T 15	Conducting instrumental groups
T 16	Helping to perform a steady beat
T 17	Putting instruments away

Ongoing skills

'Ongoing skills' are identified by the QCA scheme of work as those skills which need to be continually developed and revisited. This is in addition to the activities in the six units. The QCA suggests that learning may take place as the opportunity arises throughout the school week, eg in short 5-minute sessions.

Music Express does not include a separate Ongoing skills unit, but addresses the skills throughout its activities. When using *Music Express* as a scheme, you will be fulfilling the learning objectives and outcomes of the QCA Ongoing skills unit.

If you teach music in one weekly lesson, as opposed to three shorter lessons, you may like to select activities from *Music Express* for supplementary 5-minute activities. By doing this, you will reinforce more regularly the development of the musical skills identified by the QCA.

Extension and future learning

A & C Black website

Music Express provides all the resources you will need for teaching a year of music. We hope, however, that you will use other songs and activities to ring the changes in subsequent years or to link with other National Curriculum subjects.

The website www.acblack.com/musicexpress lists the *Music Express* activities that were drawn from or inspired by other A & C Black books, and links to other books that will supplement the activities in *Music Express.*

SOUNDS LONG SHORT LONG

1 **Sing *Some sounds are short* and make sequences of long and short vocal sounds**

- Show the children the *Long short long* cards. Explain that the long and short lines indicate long and short sounds. Play the CD and ask the children to say which of the cards is represented:

Vs1   Some sounds are short,
       Some sounds are long,
       Which sounds are on the card
       After this song?

(card 3 is represented)

Vs2   Some sounds are short,
       Some sounds are long,
       These sounds were on the card
       After the song.

(card 3 sounds are repeated)

Were the children able to identify the card? If not, ask different children to demonstrate with vocal sounds the long and short patterns on all the cards. Play the CD until the card is identified.

- Use the CD to teach the song then play this game.

  Sit in a circle. Place the *Long short long* cards in a cloth bag and pass the bag round the ring while you all sing the first verse. Whoever holds the bag at the end of the first verse picks a card from it and makes vocal sounds to match the pattern.

  Did the sounds match the pattern on the card? - discuss and improve if necessary. Ask the class, at a signal from you, to repeat the pattern all together. If the child agrees that they have performed it correctly, all sing the second verse followed by the pattern.

- Play again.

> ## Teaching tip
> Encourage the children to use a range of long and short vocal sounds, eg aaaa, woooo, deeeee, hmmm, bip, pop, etc.

3 **Accompany *Jackass wid him long tail* with a long-short action sequence**

- Listen to the CD and invite the children to 'stroke' the jackass' tail then tap their palms each time they hear the words, 'long tail'.

- All join in singing the chorus, adding the actions to 'long tail':

Jackass wid him long tail,
Bag a coco comin down.

2 **Recognise long and short vocal sounds in *Dipidu***

- All listen to the CD and notice that the song has two contrasting sections.

1   Good day, good day to you,
     Good day, oh dipidu.
     Good day, good day to you,
     Good day, oh dipidu.

2   Dip, dip, dipidu,
     Dipidu, oh dipidu,
     Dip, dip, dip, dip, dipidu,
     Dipidu, oh dipidu.

- Focusing on the long and short word sounds, ask the class about the differences between the sections, eg:

  – which section of the song has mostly long-sounding words? *(The first one - good, day, to, you, oh.)*

  – which words or syllables in section 2 sound the shortest? *(Dip, di-, -pi-)*

  – what happens in the last part of the second section? *(The sounds are even shorter and faster - 'dip dip dip dip'.)*

- Teach the song, emphasising the long sounds by singing smoothly with long vowel sounds. Emphasise the short sounds by making the syllables light and clipped.

The long and the short of it
Exploring duration

Long short long

Music Express Year 2 © A & C Black 2002
www.acblack.com/musicexpress

PLAY LONG AND SHORT

1 **Accompany *Dipidu* with long and short instrumental sounds**

- Revise *Dipidu* together, singing it with or without the CD (*track 2*).

- Sing the first section, all clapping this steady beat (*track 4*):

Good day, good day to you,

Good day, oh dipi - du.

- Invite a small group to select instruments which make long sounds (*cymbal and soft beater, triangle, bell*), and play them on the clapped beat, while the others sing (*track 5*):

Good day, good day to you ...

- Sing the second section, all lightly clapping the rhythm of the words (*track 6*):

Dip, dip, di - pi du ...

- Invite a small group to select instruments which make short sounds (*woodblocks, claves, finger castanets*), and play them to the clapped word rhythms, while the others sing (*track 7*):

Dip, dip, di - pi du ...

- Perform the song like this, with or without backing track 8:

  - beat group plays in section 1;

  - rhythm group plays in section 2;

  - everyone else claps and sings both sections.

2 **Sing *Some sounds are short* and make sequences of long and short instrumental sounds**

- All sit in a circle with a tambour, cymbal, woodblock, chime bar, and one rubber headed beater in the centre. Place the *Long short long* cards in a cloth bag and pass it round the circle while you sing the first verse.

  The child holding the bag at the end, picks a card and selects one of the instruments.

  Ask the class to suggest ways of producing on the chosen instrument:

  - a long sound (*eg slide the beater across the skin of a tambour*);

  - a short sound (*eg quickly stop a cymbal ringing by touching it*).

  The child uses the suggestions to create the pattern of sounds on the card.

  Ask the class whether the sounds matched the card and discuss how to improve the match if necessary.

  All sing the second verse. The child with the instrument plays the pattern again at the end.

- Repeat the game until each instrument has been played and a variety of techniques for playing long and short sounds have been found.

3 **Accompany *Jackass wid him long tail* with a long-short instrumental sequence**

- Ask the class to select long and short sounds on a range of instruments, eg long scraper sound then short tap, long slide on a tambour then short tap. Invite a small group of children to play. As the class sing the chorus, the players make long-short sound sequences on the instruments each time 'long tail' is repeated:

long tail

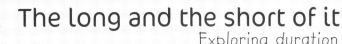
LONG TAIL, SHORT TEMPER

1 **Focus on the long and short sounds in** *Tinga layo*

- All listen to the CD, focusing on the words. Ask the children which word has the longest sound in it? *(Lay----o.)*

- Play the CD again, inviting the children to join you as you draw an arc in the air then tap your palm each time 'lay-o' is sung:

lay————————o

- Ask the children to notice the 'clip clop' sound of the donkey's hooves in the section beginning 'me donkey walk ...' Are the sounds long or short? *(Short.)* Ask if the words in this section make long or short sounds. *(Mostly short.)* Mark the short 'clip clop' sounds by tapping hands lightly on alternate knees.

clip   clop   clip   clop

2 **Learn to sing** *Tinga layo*

- Teach the song with or without the CD.

Ch Tinga layo, come, little donkey, come,
    Tinga layo, come, little donkey, come.

Vs1 Me donkey eat, me donkey sleep,
    Me donkey kick wid him two hind feet. *(x2)*

Ch Tinga layo, come, little donkey, come ...

Vs2 Me donkey walk, me donkey talk,
    Me donkey eat with a spoon and fork. *(x2)*

Ch Tinga layo, come, little donkey, come ...

- Sing the song, contrasting the long and short vocal sounds by singing them smoothly or snappily respectively.

3 **Learn word rhythms from** *Tinga layo*

- Show the children the *Tinga layo rhythms* photocopiable. Demonstrate each line by tapping and saying its rhythm *(reference track 11)*. Invite individual children to clap the rhythm of each line.

- As a class, tap alternate hands on knees and say the top line out loud *(this is the clip clop beat from activity 1)*.

  Divide the class in half. While the first half continue to say and tap the clip clop beat over and over, the second half say and tap the next line – 'tinga layo'.

  Say and tap each of the word rhythms in this way, repeating each one until everyone is joining in confidently. Swap halves.

- Invite an individual to choose one of the rhythms. Ask the class to gently tap the beat, while this child says and claps the rhythm.

  Repeat with different children performing different rhythms.

Tinga layo rhythms

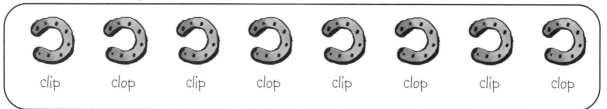

clip clop clip clop clip clop clip clop

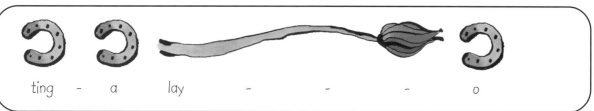

ting - a lay - - - o

spoon - and fork spoon - and fork

come lit - tle don - key come lit - tle don - key

MORE LONG TAILS

1 Identify sequences of long and short sounds in the *Tinga layo rhythms*

p12 12

- Show the children the *Tinga layo rhythms* photocopiable and ask them to notice how each rhythm is a sequence of long and short sounds, eg 'tinga layo' makes the sequence: short short long short. (*The children may like to notice that some symbols indicate even shorter sounds than others.*)

- Ask the class to suggest some other words which make sequences of long and short sounds.

  They may use words from the song, eg 'me donkey', or invent their own, eg 'hee haw' or 'very long ears'.

- Say and tap the new rhythms as a class (*reference track 12*). Emphasise the long and short sounds with your voices and with actions, eg

hee haw ——

- As a class, find ways to represent your new sequences in the blank spaces on the photocopiable. Use the hoof, tail and carrot symbols or make up your own.

2 Accompany *Tinga layo* with instruments playing sequences of long and short

13-14

- As a class, select one type of instrument to play each sequence of long-short sounds in the *Tinga layo rhythms* photocopiable, eg

  – 'tinga lay-o' (*short short long short*): Tibetan bells clapped together on short, and allowed to ring on long;

  – 'spoon and fork' (*short short long*): scraper struck on short, scraped on long;

  – 'he haw' (*short long*): cymbal tapped with a brush on short and brushed on long.

  – 'come little donkey' (*short and very short*): claves

- All listen to track 13, which shows how the rhythms may be added to the song. Ask the children what they notice. (*A bell accompanies the words 'tinga layo' whenever they are sung in the chorus; each verse is accompanied throughout by the clip clop beat and one of the other word rhythms.*)

  Ask them to identify which word rhythm accompanies each verse. (*Answer: vs 1 – 'spoon and fork', vs 2 – 'come little donkey'.*)

- Select three small groups and perform the song like this to track 14:

  – group 1: 'tinga layo' – play the chosen instruments on the words 'tinga layo' in the chorus;

  – group 2: select any other rhythm and its instrument and play throughout verse 1;

  – group 3: select any other rhythm and its instrument and play throughout verse 2;

  – everyone listens and taps the clip clop beat.

- Evaluate the performance, and discuss improvements, eg

  – did the rhythm groups play in time?

  – do you need a conductor to signal when to begin?

  – were the long-short sequences clearly heard?

- Repeat with different children playing the rhythms.

3 Listen to *Mi caballo blanco* and mark long and short sounds with actions

15

- All listen to the CD. Ask the children what the song is about. (*A horse and its rider.*) All practise tapping the rhythm of the words 'mi caballo' (*'my horse'*) each time they are sung:

Mi   ca – bal – lo

Ask if this rhythm pattern is made up of short or long sounds? (*Short.*)

- Ask the children which of the song words have the longest sounds. (*Se vay se va.*) Draw an arc in the air on each of these words:

Se – vay – se – va

Background information

- 'Mi caballo' means 'my horse', and 'galopando va' means 'gallop away'.
- The song is by the renowned Chilean composer Francisco Flores del Campo.

FOUR-LEGGED FRIENDS

1 **Listen to galloping rhythms in *The jockeys' dance***

• Listen to track 16 and ask the children to suggest which animal is being represented by the music. (*Horse.*)

• Listen again and ask the children to join in with the galloping horse's hooves by tapping the beat on alternate knees.

• Ask whether the hoof sounds are long or short. (*Short.*) Ask what material they think the instrument playing these sounds is made from. (*Wood.*)

Background information

• *The jockey's dance* comes from Eleanor Alberga's orchestral setting of Roald Dahl's *Revolting Rhyme, Snow-White and the Seven Dwarfs.* It depicts a race scene in which the seven dwarfs (the jockeys) bet all their money on a horse.

Teaching tip

• Some children will find it helpful to tap the beat with fingers on palms as they sing.

2 **Learn to sing *Mi caballo blanco,* focusing on the beat and the word rhythms**

• Use track 17 to teach the children this action pattern which marks the beat and prepares a matching drum pattern:

• Teach the children the song words using track 18 (*words sung at a slower tempo*). Concentrate on saying the words clearly and matching the rhythms accurately:

Vs As brilliant as the sunrise,
My horse is white as snow,
A friend that's ever faithful,
Riding together we will go.

Ch Mi caballo, mi caballo,
Galopando va,
Mi caballo, mi caballo,
Galopando va.
Se – vay – se – va.
Se – vay – se – va, mm.

(*Repeat from the beginning.*)

• When this is secure, all sing along to track 15, adding the drum beat actions to the chorus.

3 **Listen to *Mi caballo blanco* and identify the accompanying instruments**

• Give each child a copy of the photocopiable chart below. All listen to the CD and, as you name each section for them, the children tick the instruments they hear. Play the CD as often as needed.

	Introduction	Verse	Chorus	Verse	Chorus

• Ask the class to name the instrument which plays the 'mi caballo' rhythm which they tapped earlier. (*Two-tone woodblock.*) Which instrument plays the 'Se vay se va' pattern? (*Chime bars.*)

GALLOPING AWAY

1 Sing *Mi caballo blanco* and learn the instrumental accompaniments

- Divide the class into three groups, one for each of the body percussion patterns learnt in previous lessons:

  - tap 'white as snow' throughout the chorus.
  - tap alternate knees on 'mi caballo'
  - draw arcs on 'se vay se va'

  Give each group practice at playing their pattern while everyone else sings. Swap the patterns round until each group is secure with all three. Finally, perform all three patterns at once to track 18.

- Transfer the three patterns onto percussion:

  - select a small group to play the 'white as snow' beat on hand drums, tapping the centre firmly and the edge lightly:

  - select a group to play 'mi caballo' on claves:

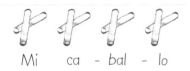

  - select another group to play chime bars on 'se vay se va':

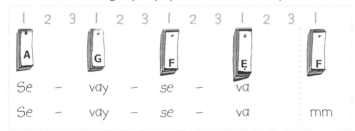

- Give the players time and space to practise adding their pattern to track 18.

3 Put on a class concert entitled *Four-legged friends*

- Revise the songs and accompaniments the class have learnt in this unit, and decide on a running order for a class concert. Invite a volunteer to present the concert. The presenter introduces each four-legged friend in turn and invites the class to sing 'Dipidu' in welcome, eg

  - 'Ladies and gentlemen, will you please give a warm welcome to our friend the jackass' – all sing *Dipidu*;
  - play the *Jackass wid him long tail* CD track 9 and perform the long-short actions and sounds;
  - presenter introduces the donkey – all sing *Dipidu*;
  - sing *Tinga layo* and accompany with instruments;
  - presenter introduces the horse – all sing *Dipidu*;
  - sing *Mi caballo blanco* and accompany as above.

2 Perform *Mi caballo blanco* with voices and percussion

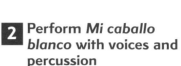

- Using first track 18 then the faster track 15, revise the song as a class, concentrating on singing the words clearly and in rhythm.

- Divide each of the percussion groups from activity 1 in half: a singing half and a playing half. Group all the singers together, and practise singing the song three times, adding one percussion group each time.

  Swap the halves so that everyone has practice playing and singing.

- Make a cassette recording of two performances (*one of each half*). Evaluate the performances as a class, and all suggest possible improvements.

- As a class, discuss other possible arrangements of the song, eg consider

  - whether to play the 'white as snow' pattern throughout the song or only during the chorus;
  - where else to play the 'mi caballo' pattern eg introduction and verse;
  - including the 'se vay se va' pattern in the introduction.

Teaching tips

Help the chime bar group play their part by:

• ensuring that they bounce the beaters off the bars to make a long ringing sound;

• suggesting that they tap beats 2 and 3 in the air –

Feel the pulse
Exploring pulse and rhythm

STEP RUN JUMP

1 **Sing *Down the avenue* and move, sing and clap at different speeds**

- All listen to the CD. Ask the children to notice how the music changes in each verse. *(It is slow in the first verse, faster in the second and even faster in the third.)*

- Invite the children to move around the room as they listen again, matching their steps to the speed (*tempo*) of the music.

- Teach the children the song, verse by verse.

Vs1   Grandpa's strolling down the avenue,
       Grandpa's strolling down the avenue,
       Grandpa's strolling down the avenue,
       Strolling down the avenue with me.

Vs2   Grown-ups striding down the avenue ...
       Striding down the avenue with me.

Vs3   My friend's running down the avenue ...
       Running down the avenue with me.

- Clap the beat of one of the verses. The children listen, then say which verse matches the tempo you have clapped. Invite a child to lead.

Teaching tip

- This is an energetic action song. Give the children a strong lead, performing the actions with vigour in order to mark the beat clearly.

3 **Sing the action song, *Kye kye kule***

- Explain that *Kye kye kule* is a call and response song. Invite the children to join in with the responses as they listen to the CD.

Call: *Response:*
Kye kye kule,   Kye kye kule,
Kye kye kofi nsa,   Kye kye kofi nsa,
Kofi nsa langa,   Kofi nsa langa,
Kaka shi langa,   Kaka shi langa,
Kum adende,   Kum adende.
          All: Kum adende. Hey!

- Sing the song (*with or without the CD*) and lead the actions, which are shown on the *Kye kye kule* photocopiable. Invite the children to copy you.

- When the actions are well established, show the children the *Kye kye kule* photocopiable. Explain that the actions are performed to the regular beat of the song. Sing the song together without doing the actions; instead, point to each action symbol on the beat as you sing the words.

  Invite individual children to point to the beat as the others sing.

Teaching tip

- If space is limited, two children may act out the movement while the others join in tapping hands on knees. Alternatively, all step on the spot.

2 **Listen to *March past of the kitchen utensils***

- All listen to the CD and 'march' to the beat with alternate fists on knees.

- Ask the children if the beat changes speed. *(No, it stays at the same steady tempo throughout.)*

- Listen again and ask a small group to stand in line, and march their feet in time to the beat (*on the spot if you do not have room to move about*). As they march, the class join in with fists on knees and notice how well the marchers are moving their feet in time.

Background information

- The British composer, Vaughan Williams (1872-1958), wrote this music for a student play. It describes kitchen utensils coming to life, marching around the kitchen and occasionally crashing into each other.

Kye Kye Kule

1	2	3	4	1	2	3	4

Call *Response*

Kye   kye   ku - le   Kye   kye   ku - le

Kye kye ko - fi'n - sa   Kye kye ko-fi'n - sa

Kofi'n - sa lan - ga   Kofi'n - sa lan - ga

Kaka   shi lan - ga   Kaka   shi lan - ga

Kum   a - den - de   Kum   a - den - de

All

Kum   a - den - de   HEY!

Music Express Year 2 © A & C Black 2002
www.acblack.com/musicexpress

17

BEAT AND RHYTHM

1 Sing *Someone's in the kitchen with Dinah* and mark the beat and the rhythm with actions

- Use the CD to teach the song and all mime strumming a banjo to the beat during the chorus:

Strum - ming on   the old   ban - jo

Ch   Someone's in the kitchen with Dinah,
      Someone's in the kitchen I know I know,
      Someone's in the kitchen with Dinah,
      Strumming on the old banjo.

Vs   Fee, fie, fiddle-ee-i-o,
      Fee, fie, fiddle-ee-i-o,
      Fee, fie, fiddle-ee-i-o,
      Strumming on the old banjo.

- All practise these verse actions slowly without the CD, but keeping a steady beat. On the words 'fee', 'fie' and 'fiddle-ee-i-o', mime playing the flute, clarinet and violin respectively:

fee   fie   fid - dle - ee - i - o

When the children can coordinate the actions and words at this tempo, practise at a faster speed.

- Perform the song with the CD, adding the chorus and verse actions throughout.

2 Play *Beat or rhythm?* with *Kye kye kule*

- Play track 23, in which the *Kye kye kule* singers are accompanied by a drum tapping the beat. Play the track again and ask the children to clap the beat as you point to the action symbols on the photocopiable.

- Play track 24, in which the singers are accompanied by a drum tapping the word rhythms. Ask the children to say why this version is different. (*The rhythm is tapped, not the steady beat.*) All sing and clap the word rhythms. (*Check that the children can do this accurately.*)

- Show the children enlarged photocopies of the *Beat* and *Rhythm* cards below. Explain that when you hold up the *Beat* card, they should sing *Kye kye kule* and clap the beat, and when you hold up the *Rhythm* card, they should sing and clap the rhythm. Practise this, checking that the children are responding appropriately.

- Now play the *Beat or rhythm?* game. All begin singing *Kye kye kule*. As soon as you hold up the *Beat* card the children respond by clapping the beat as they sing. When you change to the *Rhythm* card, they respond immediately by clapping the rhythm. Continue to alternate the cards as the children sing.

- Invite individuals to lead.

beat | rhythm

Photocopiable beat and rhythm cards to enlarge

3 Listen to *March past of the kitchen utensils* to identify beat and rhythm

- Ask the children to say whether the music begins with the beat or the rhythm. (*It begins with the beat.*)

- Ask what happens next? (*The beat and rhythm are played together.*)

Feel the pulse
Exploring pulse and rhythm
3rd

BEAT AND RHYTHM TIME

1 **Accompany *Someone's in the kitchen with Dinah* with instruments**

- Sing the song with or without the CD (track 22) and revise the actions the children learned in the last lesson.

- Select three types of untuned percussion instruments, eg tambourines, drums, bells. Divide the class into three groups and allocate one type of instrument to each. As a class devise a new verse for each instrument and change the last line of the chorus as well, eg (*reference track 25*):

Ch   Someone's in the Kitchen with Dinah ...
       Tapping on the tambourine.

Vs   Chink chink chinkety chink chink ...
       Tapping on the tambourine.

Ch   Someone's in the Kitchen with Dinah ...
       Tapping on the old skin drum.

Vs   Boom boom boombedy boom boom ...

- Choose a conductor from each group. During the chorus, the conductor mimes playing the beat on their group's instrument while the group plays the beat. During the verse, the conductor mimes and the group plays the word rhythms, eg

tambourine group - chorus:

Someone's in   the Kit- chen with   Di   –   –   nah ...
Tap-ping on   the tam - bour - rine.

tambourine group - verse:

Chink   chink   chin - Ke - ty   chink   chink...

- Perform the whole song with or without backing track 26. While one group plays, everyone else sings.

Teaching tips

- When performing in groups, bring everyone in together with a steady count, eg *One two three four Someone's in the kitchen ...*

- Help the group to keep in time with each other by tapping along with them until the beat is secure.

2 **Play *Beat or rhythm?* with familiar songs**

- Remind the children of the *Beat or rhythm?* game from the previous lesson.

- Play the game with two or three well-known songs chosen by the children, eg *This old man, I hear thunder, Okki-tokki-unga.* Choose a child to lead the game by holding up one card at a time, to which the class respond appropriately by clapping the beat or rhythm as they sing.

3 **Learn the rhythms of *What's the time, Mr Wolf?***

- Play track 27 and all join in with the chant, tapping feet on the floor on the beat throughout:

(One   two   three)   What's the time,   Mr   Wolf? (stamp)
Time   to get   up   What's the time,   Mr   Wolf? (stamp)
Time   to mow the lawn ...

- Place the *Mr Wolf* photocopiable where the children can see it. Ask the children to stamp the beat and chant the question 'What's the time, Mr Wolf?' with you, then as they continue to stamp, you clap one of the answer rhythms (*reference track 28*). Can the children tell you what time it is, eg 'Time to mow the lawn'? Continue until they have heard all the rhythms clapped like this. Explain that as soon as they hear the response, 'Dinner time', they stop stamping.

- Invite the children to stamp and chant the wolf's question and clap the answering rhythm as you point to its line on the *Mr Wolf* photocopiable. Mix up the order and repeat until the class is familiar with each clapped answer.

Mr Wolf

1	2	3	4

Time   to   get   up

Time   to   mow   the   lawn!

Time   to   wash   the   di - shes!

Din - ner time!

Music Express Year 2 © A & C Black 2002
www.acblack.com/musicexpress

DINNER TIME RHYTHMS

1 **Play *What's the time, Mr Wolf?* to practise recognising clapped word rhythms** p.20

- Revise the clapped *Mr Wolf* rhythms from Lesson 3 activity 3, checking that all the children remember which rhythm matches which answer.

- Play *What's the time, Mr Wolf?* like this:
  - the class stamp the beat throughout and ask the repeated question, 'What's the time, Mr Wolf?';
  - you take the role of Mr Wolf, clapping the rhythm but not the words of his answers or tapping them on a drum;
  - as soon as Mr Wolf taps 'Dinner time', the class stops stamping and keeps very silent or the wolf will eat them up!

- When the game is well established, invite one of the children to be Mr Wolf. Keep changing the leadership to give several children the opportunity to perform the rhythms.

3 **Invent a new class version of *A plate of potatoes***

- As a class, discuss suggestions for a new verse about a meal made with potatoes (*the words do not have to rhyme, but they do need to fit into a count of four beats*), eg

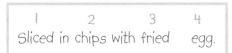

1	2	3	4
Sliced in chips with fried			egg.

- Invite a child to clap the rhythm of the new words while you tap and count the beat. Does the rhythm match the words, and do the words fit into four beats? If the class approves the rhythm, perform the chant with the new words, everyone tapping the beat of the chorus, and clapping the new rhythm as in activity 2.

- Divide into four groups. Ask each group to invent as many new verses for the chant as they like, but to select their favourite invention for a class performance. Give each group time and space to practise saying and clapping the rhythm of their words, if necessary helping them to fit their verse into a count of four beats.

- Perform the new version of *A plate of potatoes* as a class. Decide on an order for each group to perform their new verse with the clapped rhythm. All chant the chorus and tap the beat.

2 **Perform the beat and word rhythms in *A plate of potatoes***  29))

- Listen to the CD together and join in with the chorus:

    A plate of potatoes, a plate of potatoes,

Ch   There's nothing as great as a plate of potatoes!

Vs1   Baked in foil, fried in oil,

Ch   There's nothing as great as a plate of potatoes!

Vs2   Cooked in a curry, boiled in a hurry,

Ch   There's nothing as great as a plate of potatoes!

Vs3   Stewed in a pot? Give me the lot!

Ch   There's nothing as great as a plate of potatoes!

Vs4   Mushed with cheese? Mmm, yes please!

Ch   There's nothing as great as a plate of potatoes!

- As they listen to the CD again, ask the children to say whether the beat or the rhythm is being clapped during the chorus. (*The beat.*)

There's no -thing as great as a plate of po - ta - toes!

Perform the chorus together, tapping knees on the beat. Ask how many beats are tapped in the chorus. (*Four.*)

- Listen to the CD again, and ask the children to say whether the beat or the rhythm is being clapped during the verses, eg:

Vs1   Baked   in foil,   fried   in oil.

(*Answer: the rhythm*)

- Teach the verses using the CD and clapping their rhythms together.

- Perform the chant, with or without the CD, alternately tapping the beat of the chorus and clapping the rhythm of the verses.

Feel the pulse
Exploring pulse and rhythm

GET READY TO EAT

1 Accompany *A plate of potatoes* with instruments

- In the same groups as Lesson 4 activity 3, revise the new verses for the chant.

- Make available a range of percussion instruments including home-made sound makers.

  Each group selects one type of instrument which they think matches the words they have made up, eg

  - *a potato soup group might shake plastic bottles half-filled with water;*
  - *a mashed potato group might tap tambours.*

- Each group practises playing the rhythm of their verse on the instruments.

- Perform the whole chant as a class:
  - all chant the chorus and tap the beat;
  - each group in turn contributes their rhythm.

  Evaluate the performance together, eg
  - *did each group start playing on time?*
  - *did everyone maintain a steady beat?*

3 Listen and move to *Chinese kitchen*

- Listen to the CD (*after a loud introduction, the music continues more quietly to a fast steady beat*). Ask the children what instrument they can hear playing the fast steady beat. (*Small cymbals clashed together.*)

  Ask them to notice when the instrument playing the beat changes (*around 0.40*). Can they identify this instrument? (*Claves or wooden sticks.*)

- Listen to the CD again. Ask the children to join in, tapping two 'chopsticks' on the cymbal and claves beat (*tap two fingers on the palm of the other hand*).

- Ask the children to describe what happens towards the end of the piece. (*At 1.40 the music is suddenly slower before gradually fading to finish.*)

- Invite the children to mime actions to the beat to show preparations for a meal, eg
  - *chopping cabbage;*
  - *peeling carrots;*
  - *stirring a pan or wok.*

2 Sing *How many people here for dinner?* and combine the beat and word rhythms

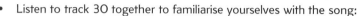

- Listen to track 30 together to familiarise yourselves with the song:

  Vs1 How many people here for dinner? (Hands up!)
       How many heard the dinner bell?
       How many people here for dinner? (Hands up!)
       Roll up! Roll up! Roll up! sniff sniff
       Mmmmmmmm! What's that smell?
       Yorkshire pudding, Yorkshire pudding. *x2*

  Vs2 How many people here for dinner ...
       Cauliflower cheese, cauliflower cheese. *x2*

  Vs3 How many people here for dinner ...
       Baked banana, baked banana. *x2*

  Vs4 How many people here for dinner? (Hands up!)
       How many heard the dinner bell?
       How many people here for dinner? (Hands up!)
       Grubs up! Grubs up! Grubs up! sniff sniff
       Mmmmmmmm! Eat up well!

- Listen again, and invite the children to tap the beat on their knees throughout:

Sing the song and tap the beat together until the children are confident with the words and melody.

- All sing the first verse, but continue quietly repeating 'Yorkshire pudding, Yorkshire pudding' until you signal stop. Repeat, this time saying and tapping the rhythm of 'Yorkshire pudding' with fingers on palms.

  Divide the class in half. Explain that the first half will go back to the beginning of the verse and sing it again, while the second half continues to say and tap 'Yorkshire pudding'. End together on 'Mmmmmmmm! What's that smell' (*reference track 31*).

  Practise performing the other verses in the same way.

- Divide into four groups and perform the song like this:
  - all sing the first verse;
  - group 1 continues to say and tap 'Yorkshire pudding', while everyone else goes on to the next verse;
  - group 2 continues to say and tap 'Cauliflower cheese', while the others go on to the next verse;
  - group 3 continues to say and tap 'Baked banana' while group 4 sings the last verse. Everyone stops on 'Eat up well!' (*reference track 32*).

Feel the pulse
Exploring pulse and rhythm
6th

EAT UP WELL

1 Perform *How many people here for dinner?* layering the word rhythms on instruments

30))

- Revise the song using CD track 30. All tap the beat throughout. Choose three children to play the beat on instruments. Ask them to find a sound which represents setting a table with plates (*eg agogo bells, real plates tapped with a drumstick ...*).

  All sing the song accompanied by the beat.

- Divide into the four groups from Lesson 5 activity 2, and ask groups 1, 2 and 3 to choose three different types of instrument – one for each food rhythm. Group 4 plays the beat.

  Give each group practise playing their rhythm, while group 4 sings the song. Check that the volume of playing does not overpower the singing.

- Finally, perform the song all through, each group adding their instrumental rhythm until all are combined into three layers as in Lesson 5 activity 2.

- Swap the groups round to give the singers an opportunity to play.

3 Perform *Dinner time*

- Prepare the class for the *Dinner time* performance, eg checking that everyone knows their role in each section, that the groups have their instruments ready, and Mr Wolf has his prompt card. If you are using backing tracks, appoint a sound manager to control the CD player and ensure that the backing tracks are played in the correct order.

- Run through the performance and evaluate its success. What might be improved?

  – Is everyone listening to the steady beat and playing in time with each other?

  – Are the sections following on from each other without unnecessary gaps?

  – Are the instrumental groups layering their sounds clearly and controlling the volume?

- Perform *Dinner time* at an assembly about food.

2 Rehearse a performance of *Dinner time*

- Explain to the children that you are going to put together a performance called *Dinner time*, which may include any of the activities already explored. Make your selection together and write the running order on the board, eg:

  What's the time, Mr Wolf?
  Time to make the dinner.

  Chinese kitchen mime

  What's the time, Mr Wolf?
  Time to set the knives and forks

  How many people here for dinner?

  What's the time, Mr Wolf?
  Dinnertime!

  A plate of potatoes

  What's the time, Mr Wolf?
  Time to wash the dishes ...
  (Groan!)

- Discuss how you will organise the performance. Consider:

  – whether to use CD backing tracks

  – whether to have a conductor who brings everyone in together for the Mr Wolf chants by counting and stamping 'one two three';

  – whether all or just a few performers will mime the Chinese kitchen scene, while the other quietly tap the beat on their instruments;

  – whether to stay in the same four groups for *How many people here for dinner?* and *A plate of potatoes*. If so, which instruments will be needed.

  – how to end the performance with a flourish, eg the *Mr Wolf* conductor holds up a large prompt card saying 'groan'

JUMP ALL AROUND

1 **Demonstrate pitch movement in *I jump out of bed in the morning* with whole body movements**

- Play track 34 and ask the children to listen carefully to the melody each time the words 'I jump' are sung.

  I jump out of bed in the morning,
  I jump out of bed in the morning,
  I jump out of bed in the morning,
  I hope it's a very nice day.

  Ask whether the melody is the same each time? *(No, the melody jumps higher each time 'I jump' is sung.)*

- Listen to track 34 again, all making a small, a medium and a high jump with hands or with whole bodies to match the three jumps in the melody.

- Play track 35 *(cumulative action verses)*. Join in with the singing, and add the jumping actions and new actions in each verse.

  What do the children notice about each verse? *(The verses get longer as more actions are added.)*

  Ask what happens when a new action is added – does the melody go up, down, or stay on the same note? *(It stays on the same note.)*

3 **Listen to *Six little ducks that I once knew* and play a notation game** p24 **37**

- All listen to the CD and notice the three quacks which are repeated three times at the end of the song. Join in with this quack melody.

  Ask whether the three quacks move up, down, or stay at the same pitch. *(They move down.)*

  Ask whether they jump or move by step? *(They move by step.)*

- Display the three quack cards on the board, placing them as illustrated here to show the notes of the melody. All sing the descending quack pattern.

  Now move the cards so that they are vertically further apart. Invite children to make high, medium and low quacks with their voices to match the new relative positions. Invite a child to adjust the cards for the class to interpret, trying different orders of high, medium and low sounds.

2 **Sing *Looby Loo* and identify pitch movement** p25 **36**

- Listen to the CD:

  Ch   Here we go Looby Loo,
        Here we go Looby Light,
        Here we go Looby Loo,
        All on a Saturday night.

  Vs1   First the tune jumps up,
        Then it turns around,
        Then it goes jogging and jumping,
        Then it steps all the way down.

  Ch   Here we go Looby Loo,
        Here we go Looby Light,
        Here we go Looby Loo,
        All on a Saturday night.

  Vs2   First your hand jumps up,
        Then it turns around,
        Then it goes jogging and jumping,
        Then it steps all the way down.

- All join in singing the song, making the hand movements indicated by the words in the second verse.

- Show the children the *Looby Loo lines* photocopiable which shows the pitch shape of each line of the melody. All sing the first verse. Point to each chime bar on the photocopiable as its note is sung.

  Ask individual children to describe the shape of each line, eg

  – line 1: the tune jumps up in the middle and then jumps up higher at the end.

Photocopiable quack cards

Looby Loo lines

First   the   tune   jumps   up

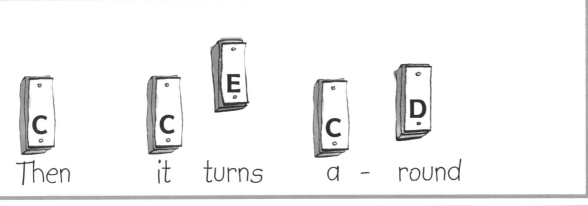

Then   it   turns   a - round

Then   it   goes   jog - ging   and   jump -ing

Then   it   steps   all   the   way   down

Music Express Year 2 © A & C Black 2002
www.acblack.com/musicexpress

HIGH LOW QUACKERS

1 **Sing *Six little ducks that I once knew***
and use instruments and whole bodies p27 37))
to demonstrate pitch movement

• Teach the song. As you sing the words 'quack quack quack', point in turn to each 'quack' on the *Quackers* photocopiable:

Six little ducks that I once knew,
Fat ones, skinny ones, they were too.
But the one little duck with the feathers on his back,
He ruled the others with his
    Quack quack quack,
    Quack quack quack.
He ruled the others with his
    Quack quack quack.

• Invite a small group to accompany the 'quacks' with chime bars:

quack quack quack

• Invite another group to devise movements which match the quacks (*eg flapping elbows and bending knees to move the body lower on each quack*).

• Perform the song with the chime bar and dance accompaniment.

2 **Improvise *Jazzyquacks* music to**
enjoy playing with pitch movement p27 38))

• Show the class the *Jazzyquacks* photocopiable. All listen to the CD together and ask the children these questions:

   – which picture matches the first ducks you hear? (*1 – descending ducks.*)

   – which picture matches the highest sounds you hear? (*2 – baby ducks.*)

   – all silently raise hands when you hear the big duck dancing.

   – which two cards are heard together? (*1 and 2.*)

   – when are all the ducks heard together? (*At the end.*)

• Place one or two glockenspiels or xylophones in a quiet, separate space along with enlarged copies of the *Jazzyquacks* cards (*make two or three copies of each*). Invite the children, singly or in pairs to improvise their own *Jazzyquacks* music on the instruments.

3 **Play *Listen, Looby***
Loo* to focus on p25 36))
pitch movement

• Revise the song, all singing it with the CD.

• Play one of the *Looby Loo lines* from the photocopiable on a xylophone or chime bars. Ask the children to show you which line you have played by making the matching hand movements.

• Invite a child to select and play one of the lines for the class to identify with its matching hand movements.

Quackers

 quack

 quack

 quack

Jazzyquacks

1

2

3

FOSSIL FEET

Photocopiable footprint •

1 Listen to pitch movement in *The prehistoric animal brigade*

- Ask the children to listen to the CD, then say what happens to each new verse. *(It is the same melody each time, but each verse sounds higher than the one before.)*

Vs1   Listen to the chorus
      Of the brontosaurus,
      And the stegosaurus,
      Down by the swamp.

Vs2   Along comes the dinosaur,
      Making such a loud roar,
      Thumping with his feet
      And going stomp, stomp, stomp.

Vs3   Pterodactyl flapping,
      Long beak clacking,
      Big teeth snapping,
      Down from the tree.

Vs4   Here's a woolly mammoth,
      Tusks all curly,
      Joins the hurly burly,
      Oh dear me!

      What a noise!
      It's the boys
      Of the prehistoric animal brigade!

- Teach the song and add these actions on the beat:

    – verse 1: tap knees
    – verse 2: tap hips
    – verse 3: tap chest
    – verse 4: tap head
    – ending ('What a noise ...'): stamp feet and wave arms.

2 Make a score of *The prehistoric animal brigade* melody

- All listen to verse 1 of the song on track 40. Ask the children to describe the pitch movement of the first line, 'Listen to the chorus'. *(It jumps down twice and then jumps back up.)*

Ask what they notice about the second and third lines. *(They are the same as the first line.)*

Ask what happens to the last line of the melody. *(It steps up and back again.)*

- All sing the first verse of the song, using hands to show the pitch movement of the melody.

- Make twenty-two enlarged footprint cards from the one above.

Sing the first line of the song then invite a child to attach six of the footprints to the classroom board to show the pitch movement.

(Answer:)

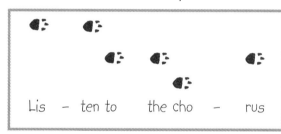

If the class are satisfied that the footprints match the melody shape, attach the footprints for the next two lines, which are the same.

Now sing the last line, asking a child to place the remaining four footprints.

(Answer:)

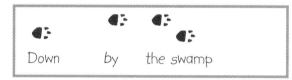

- Choose a conductor to point to each footprint on the score as you all perform the first verse. *(A complete score is given on the CD-ROM.)*

3 Listen to *Fossils* and notice pitch differences in the melody

- All listen to the *Fossils* melody on track 41. All notice that it is in two sections which are almost identical. Ask which instrument plays the first section? *(Xylophone.)* Which plays the second section? *(Piano.)*

Ask how the second section differs from the first? *(It ends differently. The notes of the first ending step down. The notes of the second ending jump up.)*

- Listen to Saint-Saens' orchestral arrangement of the melody on track 42. All count how many times the complete melody is performed. *(Five times: 1 xylophone–piano; 2 xylophone–piano; orchestral interlude; 3 xylophone–piano; 4 xylophone–piano; orchestral interlude; 5 full orchestra playing both sections.)*

Background information

- *Fossils* is a section from *The carnival of the animals* by the French composer, Saint-Saens (1835-1921). The complete work is a zoological fantasy in fourteen sections, each representing a different animal.

PATTERNS IN THE ROCK

1 Perform *The prehistoric animal brigade* with a drone accompaniment

- Revise the song, performing the actions from Lesson 3 activity 1 on the beat.

- Give chime bars to four children (*notes* F G A B♭). Ask them to line up in any order. Signal each child to play their chime bar in turn. The class instructs individual children to move place until they have ordered the notes from left to right and from lowest to highest:

- Show the class an enlarged copy of the ***What a noise!*** photocopiable arranged as shown on the CD-ROM. Notice the way each verse steps up.

- As a class, sing the first verse of the song. The first child in the row plays chime bar F on the beat throughout - a drone accompaniment:

F	F	F	F	F	F	F	F
Listen to the chor - us				of the bronto-sau - rus ...			

- Repeat for the other three verses, the second, third and fourth children playing drones on G, A and B♭ respectively.

  End with all four chime bars playing the beat together while the class stamp feet and wave:

*	*	*	*	*	*	*
What a noise!				It's the boys ...		

- Decide together on an introduction to the song (eg the F chime bar player taps four times on the beat).

- Use the score to direct a performance of ***What a noise***, (reference track 43.)

3 Perform *Fossils in the rock* with a drone accompaniment

- All listen to the *Fossils* song on track 45. Ask the children what is different about the arrangement. (*A drone accompaniment has been added on tuned percussion.*)

  Ask how many notes the tuned percussion instrument plays at once? (*Two.*) Are they the same or different? (*They are different.*)

  Invite volunteers to sing one or other of the drone notes. Using a xylophone (*alto preferably*), encourage the children to sing the drone notes again and find them on the instrument. (*They are notes C and G.*)

- Select a small group to play the drone accompaniment on tuned instruments, while the rest of the class sing the song. (*The drone is given on the photocopiable.*)

2 Sing *Fossils in the rock* and notice how the pitch moves

- Teach the song using the *Fossils in the rock* photocopiable and track 44 (*show the children how to navigate the score to go to the different endings*):

Section 1 Fossils in the rock
           Pterydactyl teeth
           Millions of years
           Made an ammonite.

Section 2 Fossils in the rock
           Pterydactyl teeth
           Millions of years
           Made an ammonite.

- Encourage the children to look carefully at the pattern of chime bar notes on the score as they listen to or sing the first section. Ask the children to describe in words or by moving their hands in the air how the pattern of the first line moves in pitch. (*The melody jumps up, down, then moves up by step.*)

- Ask what is different about the second and third lines. (*They move in the same way as the first. The pattern is nearly identical, but each starts lower.*)

- Sing the song, showing the pitch movement with your hands.

What a noise!

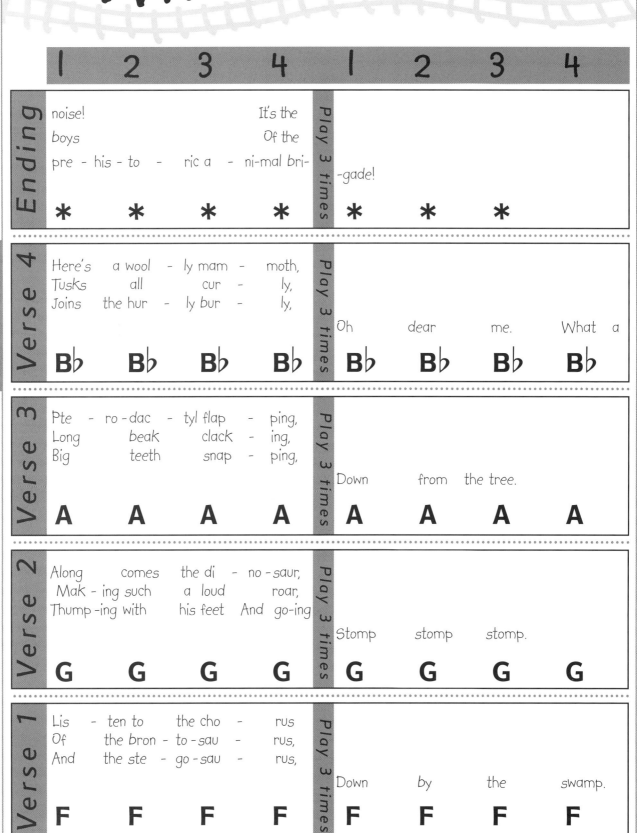

	1	2	3	4		1	2	3	4
Ending	noise!			It's the	Play 3 times				
	boys			Of the					
	pre - his - to - ric a - ni-mal bri-					-gade!			
	*	*	*	*		*	*	*	
Verse 4	Here's a wool - ly mam - moth,				Play 3 times				
	Tusks all cur - ly,								
	Joins the hur - ly bur - ly,								
						Oh	dear	me.	What a
	B♭	**B♭**	**B♭**	**B♭**		**B♭**	**B♭**	**B♭**	**B♭**
Verse 3	Pte - ro -dac - tyl flap - ping,				Play 3 times				
	Long beak clack - ing,								
	Big teeth snap - ping,								
						Down	from	the tree.	
	A	**A**	**A**	**A**		**A**	**A**	**A**	**A**
Verse 2	Along comes the di - no -saur,				Play 3 times				
	Mak - ing such a loud roar,								
	Thump -ing with his feet And go-ing								
						Stomp	stomp	stomp.	
	G	**G**	**G**	**G**		**G**	**G**	**G**	**G**
Verse 1	Lis - ten to the cho - rus				Play 3 times				
	Of the bron - to -sau - rus,								
	And the ste - go -sau - rus,								
						Down	by	the	swamp.
	F	**F**	**F**	**F**		**F**	**F**	**F**	**F**

Cut out the verse boxes and position them as shown on the CD-ROM

Fossils in the rock

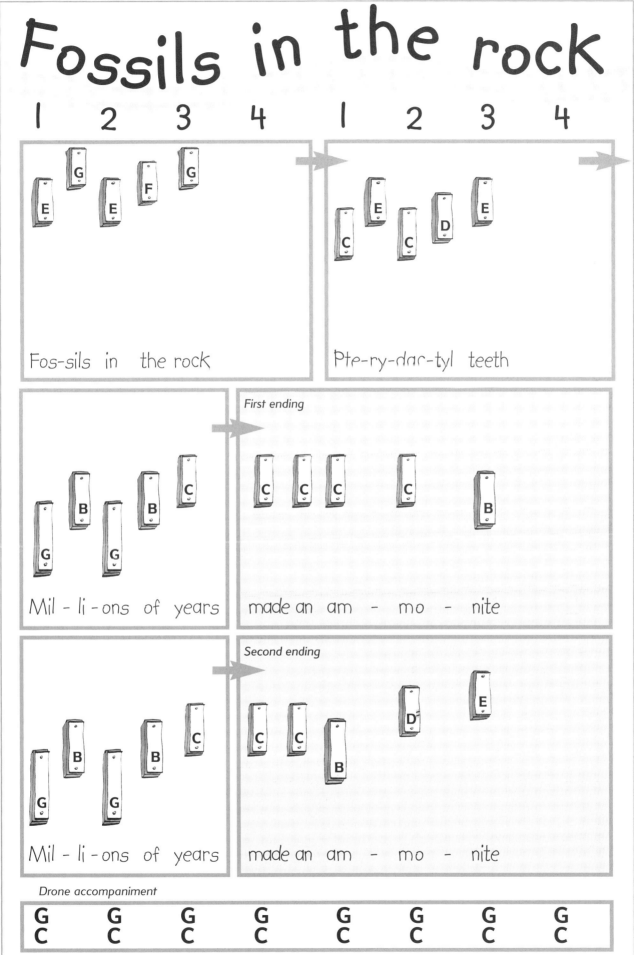

1   2   3   4   1   2   3   4

Fos-sils in the rock

Pte-ry-dar-tyl teeth

First ending

Mil - li - ons of years

made an am - mo - nite

Second ending

Mil - li - ons of years

made an am - mo - nite

Drone accompaniment

G	G	G	G	G	G	G	G
C	C	C	C	C	C	C	C

Music Express Year 2 © A & C Black 2002
www.acblack.com/musicexpress

FOSSILS ON THE MARCH

1 Plan a class arrangement of *Fossils in the rock*

- Sing the song and look at the score to remind the children of the pattern of notes which they observed in Lesson 4 activity 2. Ask what happened to the pattern each time it was played. (*It was played at a lower pitch.*)

  As a class, choose sounds to complement the high, medium and low repetitions of the pattern, eg

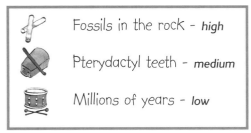

  Fossils in the rock - *high*

  Pterydactyl teeth - *medium*

  Millions of years - *low*

- Invite individual children to play the rhythm of each line of words on the chosen instrument. (*They will find it helpful to say the words silently to themselves as they play.*)

- Decide how you will accompany the words of the first and second endings – 'Made an ammonite' (*eg all the instruments might play together, or drum plays the first ending, claves the second ending*).

- Perform a class arrangement of the song. Decide together when to play and sing, eg

  – *tuned percussion drone begins and continues to the end;*
  – *singers perform both sections;*
  – *instruments perform both sections;*
  – *singers and instruments perform both sections together.*

2 Create a *Dinosaur brigade march*

- Listen to *The prehistoric animal brigade* and afterwards discuss dinosaurs with the children, collecting what facts they know about the different ones which existed.

- Ask the children to choose one of the dinosaurs from the song or from their researches and move to the beat in character. (*They may move around the room or step on the spot depending on space.*)

- Together, choose low-sounding percussion instruments to perform marching music for the 'dinosaurs', eg

  – *large drums or tambourines;*
  – *bass xylophone notes C and F;*
  – *cardboard boxes tapped with hands.*

- Select a group to practise playing the instruments to a steady beat along with the CD. (*Children with hand-held instruments may step to the beat as they play.*)

- Perform the *Dinosaur brigade march* without the CD:

  – the players begin the march music, one at a time or together;
  – the 'dinosaur' marchers join in the march one at a time, or together.

3 Use the *Fossils* melody to focus on listening

- Play this game to revise what the children have learnt about pitch and to practise their aural memory. The children perform these actions when you play the corresponding line on chime bars:

  – play the line 'Fossils in the rock' (see opposite): the children respond by curling their fists and holding them high in the air;
  – play the line, 'Pterydactyl teeth': the children point to their teeth with both index fingers;
  – play the line, 'Millions of years': the children spread their hands wide apart.

- Ask the children what they notice about the rhythm of the three melodies? (*They are the same.*) Ask the children how they can tell the difference between the three lines just by listening. (*'Fossils in the rock' is the highest-sounding, 'millions of years' is the lowest-sounding, and 'pterydactyl teeth' is in between.*)

- Hide the xylophone and play the three melodies in turn, checking that the children make the matching gestures.

  Now explain that you will play a sequence of the tunes. The children identify the higher, middle and lower versions of the melody by responding with the actions, eg

  fossils - pterydactyls - fossils - millions of years

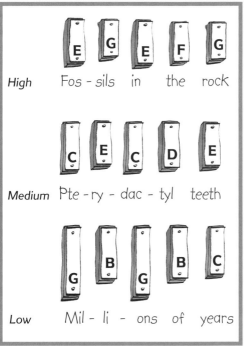

Fossils in the rock photocopiable

PREHISTORIC MUSIC SHOW

1 **Rehearse for a *Prehistoric music show***

- Explain that you are going to put on a class *Prehistoric music show*.

  Rehearse your performances of *Fossils in the rock* (as prepared in Lesson 5 activity 1), *The prehistoric animal brigade* (as in Lesson 4 activity 1) and the *Dinosaur brigade march*. Decide whether you need to use the CD backing tracks.

2 **Make a plan of the *Prehistoric music show***

- Decide as a class in which order you will perform each part of the show, eg

  - *Dinosaur brigade march*;
  - Saint-Saens' orchestral music, *Fossils*;
  - *Fossils in the rock*;
  - *The prehistoric animal brigade*.

  Make a pictorial plan of the order to remind the children, and ensure that each performance group has copies of the appropriate photocopiables if they need them for reference.

- Record and appraise together a final rehearsal of the show, eg:

  - *did the drone players keep a steady beat?*
  - *were the fossil rhythms played accurately?*
  - *was the singing clear or where any of the accompanying instruments too loud?*
  - *how can we improve our performance?*

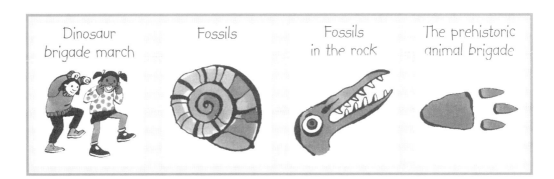

Dinosaur brigade march — Fossils — Fossils in the rock — The prehistoric animal brigade

3 **Present the *Prehistoric music show* to an audience**

- Invite volunteers to be the presenters of the show. Their responsibilities are to introduce the performers and announce the music. They might also include some of the researched information about dinosaurs in their introductions.

  Discuss with the class whether they would like their audience to participate in any way, eg clapping or tapping the beat of the march, joining in with the ending of *The prehistoric animal brigade*. If so, prime one of the presenters to explain what is required of the audience.

- Invite a younger class to watch your show.

What's the score
Exploring instruments and symbols

WOOD, METAL, SKIN

1 **Sing *Make your sound like mine* to explore a variety of sounds**

- Give each child a small hand-held shaker. All listen to the CD. At the end of each verse there is a sound for the children to copy with their shakers.

- Play the track again, pausing the CD after each verse and asking the children to describe and demonstrate each of the sounds, using the vocabulary of long, short, loud, quiet, growing louder, etc.

  Notice and discuss any interesting ways the children found to play (*eg loud - tapping the shaker firmly on the palm of the hand; long - shaking the instrument in a long gesture from left to right ...*).

- Teach the song:

  Make your sound
    the same as mine,
  The same as mine,
    the same as mine.
  Make your sound
    the same as mine,
  And make it after me!

- Invite a child to choose a way of playing their shaker (*eg fast*). All sing the song, the chosen child plays their sound, and all copy.

  Ask the class to describe the sound.

3 **Identify the instruments played in *Sextet***

- As they listen to the CD, ask the children to mime playing any instruments they hear (*eg drum, shaker, piano, clarinet, flute*).

  Can they identify the first two instruments? (*Drum and shaker.*)

  Listen again and discuss how the sounds are being produced on the instruments they recognised. (*Tapping, shaking, playing piano keys, blowing.*)

2 **Play the *Sound puzzle* game to identify different groups of instruments**

- Place a set of wooden, metal and skin instruments where all the children can see them. (*Wood might include woodblocks, claves, castanets; metal might be triangle, cymbal, agogo bell; skin might be tambour, hand drum, bongos.*) Play one of each to demonstrate its sound quality.

- All listen to the CD (*verse 2 is played three times, each time accompanied by a different set of instruments*). After verse 2 has been heard all three times, ask the children in which order they think the metal, wood and skin instruments were played. They may need to listen more than once. (*Answer: skin, metal, wood.*)

Vs1 Our sound puzzle is ready to be played,
    Our sound puzzle is ready to be played,
    Just stop and listen to every sound that's made,
    For our sound puzzle is ready to be played.

Vs2 Wood or metal, or is it made of skin?
    Wood or metal, or is it made of skin?
    Just stop and listen, your ears know how to win,
    Wood or metal, or is it made of skin?

- Practise singing the song without the CD and when it is secure, place one instrument from each set out of sight. Choose a child to select one of the hidden instruments and play the beat throughout the second verse as the class sing. Ask the children to say whether the hidden instrument was wood, metal or skin.

Teaching tips
- Keep one each of the three hidden instruments in view to remind the class of the choices available.

- To broaden the children's experience of instruments and how they are played, invite an instrumental teacher or pupil to visit and demonstrate their instruments.

FUNNY VOICES

1 **Play *Funny name game* to explore different ways of using the voice**

- Each child in turn says their name in a disguised voice, eg squeakily, slowly, loudly, grumpily, scarily. The class copy each name matching the character and sound.

- Discuss how the children changed their voices – whose voice was the quietest/ loudest/squeakiest/fastest ...

- Play the game again, each child finding a different way to disguise their voice.

2 **Play *Jamaquacks* to explore how symbols can be used to represent vocal sounds** p36

- Explain that in this circle game Jamaquacks are imaginary creatures who speak a made-up language.

  All sit in a circle. Pass a bag containing the *Jamaquacks* photocopiable cards around the circle as you say the chant:

  Jamaquack, Jamaquack, Jamaquack jive,
  Jamaquacks sing as the clock strikes five.
  One, two, three, four, five!

  The child holding the bag at the end of the chant takes a card from the bag and, keeping it hidden, turns into a Jamaquack by making a vocal sound to match the card. The other children copy the sound.

  Show the card to the children and ask whether the sound was a good match for the symbol or what improvement might be made.

- Continue the game until all cards have been placed in sequence where everyone can see them. Perform the chosen sounds one after the other, following the order shown by the cards.

3 **Play *Start conducting* to understand how symbols can be used to represent instrumental sounds** p36 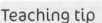 49

- All listen to the CD to familiarise yourselves with the song.

Vs 1　Pass the cards around the ring,
　　　Round the ring, round the ring,
　　　Pass the cards around the ring,
　　　You're conducting.

Vs 2　Choose a picture, put it down,
　　　Put it down, put it down,
　　　Choose another, put it down.
　　　Start conducting.

- Sit in a circle. Divide the circle into four sectors: shakers, scrapers, tappers, beaters. Give each sector appropriate instruments (eg maracas for the shakers, guiros for the scrapers, tambours for the tappers, chime bars for the beaters). Each child places their instrument on the floor in front of them.

  Show the class the four cards from the *Start conducting* photocopiable and together identify which card respresents the way each sector's instrument is played.

  As you all sing the first verse, pass the pack of four cards around the ring. The child holding the pack at the end of the verse is 'conductor' and follows the instructions given as you all sing the second verse.

  The two groups whose cards are selected, get ready to play. As the conductor points to each card in turn, the groups play freely.

> **Teaching tip**
> - The conductor decides how long to point to each card in order to indicate how long each group should play.

Jamaquacks

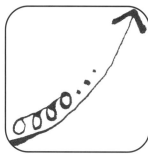
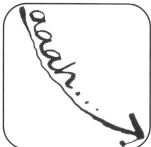

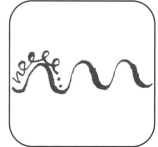

Start conducting

Shakers   *Scrapers*   *Tappers*   *Beaters*

Music Express Year 2 © A & C Black 2002
www.acblack.com/musicexpress

CARTOON VOICES

1 Use the *Jamaquacks* cards to make and perform sequences of vocal sounds p36

- Remind the children of the *Jamaquacks* game and the sounds they made with their voices in response to the picture cards.

- Sit in a circle and play the game again. At the end of the chant, the child holding the *Jamaquacks* card bag may choose up to eight cards and place them in a row in any order in front of the class.

  The conductor points to each card in turn and the class responds with its vocal sound, making it last for as long as the conductor points to the card.

- Continue the game to give other children the opportunity to be conductor and create new sequences.

  Ask whether any of the sequences were particular favourites, eg the children may have enjoyed those which ended with the laughter, or with a 'boing'.

2 Listen to *Cartoon strip* to experience how sounds can tell a story

- Play the CD then ask the children what the whole story is about. (*A trip to the park.*)

- Listen again, and ask the children what they think is happening in each short scene. All listen carefully and make a full list of everything you hear. (*The eight scenes are shown on the Cartoon strip scores photocopiable.*)

3 Use voices and body percussion to create a class improvisation of *Cartoon strip* p38

- Show the children an enlarged copy of the illustrated *Cartoon strip score* photocopiable and ask them to suggest ways of making sounds to represent each scene using their voices and body percussion.

  Make a final selection of sounds using ideas from as many children as possible.

- Perform a class improvisation of *Cartoon strip* – as you point to each scene in turn, the class respond with the selected sounds. Make a sound recording of the performance.

  Listen to the recording and evaluate its effectiveness:

  – do the sounds in each scene describe the pictures clearly?

  – were the children all making the agreed sounds?

  – should each scene be longer/shorter?

  – can every sound be heard, or should some be made more quietly, by fewer children, separately?

- Having discussed improvements, record another improvisation.

Teaching tip

- The aim is to create an improvised performance of a sequence of sound pictures which tell a story.

  The children do not need to perform in unison, but may need help in creating a texture in which individual sounds may be clearly heard.

  Encourage them to listen to each other, and be sensitive to the effect they make together, eg they might coordinate the door-closing sound, but be freer with the conversation scene.

Cartoon strip scores

What's the score?
Exploring instruments and symbols

4th

CARTOON TUNES

1 Respond to *Cartoon strip* in movement

- The children listen to track 50 or to their own recording of a *Cartoon strip* improvisation from Lesson 3 activity 3. As they listen, the children tell the story in movement. They remain seated but use their hands and arms to relate the events, eg

  – *footsteps: fists on knees;*

  – *slide: climb fist over fist, then swoop hand down ...*

  Discuss the effectiveness of the movement ideas the children have found, noticing particularly how well they synchronised with the sounds.

- In a large space, invite the children in pairs to take the parts of the two children in the cartoon strip and to practise telling the story in whole body movements - first without, then with the CD.

- Ask one pair of children to perform the story to the others as the CD plays. Let other pairs contribute their performances. Ask the watching children to notice the movement ideas which work well, and each pair's success in synchronising action with sound. Encourage the watchers to think of ways of improving their own performances.

- If there is space, invite all the pairs to perform to the CD together.

2 Use instruments to create a class improvisation of *Cartoon strip* p38

- Show the children an enlarged copy of the illustrated *Cartoon strip score* and place the blank score underneath.

  As a class, select instruments to interpret the sounds in each scene.

  Draw or write the names of the instruments on each scene of the blank score.

- Divide into eight groups – one for each of the scenes – and allocate the chosen instruments. Give each group time and space in which to practise improvising music to tell their part of the story.

- Perform the class improvisation. Choose one child to conduct the groups. This child points to each scene in turn and the groups respond with their rehearsed music.

  Assess the effectiveness of the music as you did in Lesson 3 activity 3.

- Choose two children to enact the story while the groups play.

3 Play *Hairy scary sounds matching game* p40

- Explain that the children are going to hear another set of sounds which tell a story. As they listen to the CD, ask the children to think about where the story might be taking place. (*In the rooms of a scary house or a haunted castle.*)

  Ask which sound occurs more than once, and separates all the other sounds. (*Squeaky door effect.*)

- Show the children the *Hairy Scary rooms* photocopiable. Ask the children which room they think is not represented in the recording. (*The ghost card - 'Boo'.*) Discuss the occupants or objects in the rooms and the sounds they might make.

- Give each child a copy of the photocopiable. Explain that, as they listen to the CD again, they need to order the rooms on the photocopiable to match what they hear by numbering the rooms from one to seven, omitting the ghost room.

  When this is done, play the CD again and say the order so that the children can check their answers (*order: skeletons, bats, rats, clock, creaky stairs, banging doors, wind*). Anyone who has all seven cards in the correct order may call 'Boo!' Play again until everyone calls 'Boo!'.

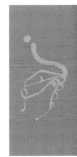

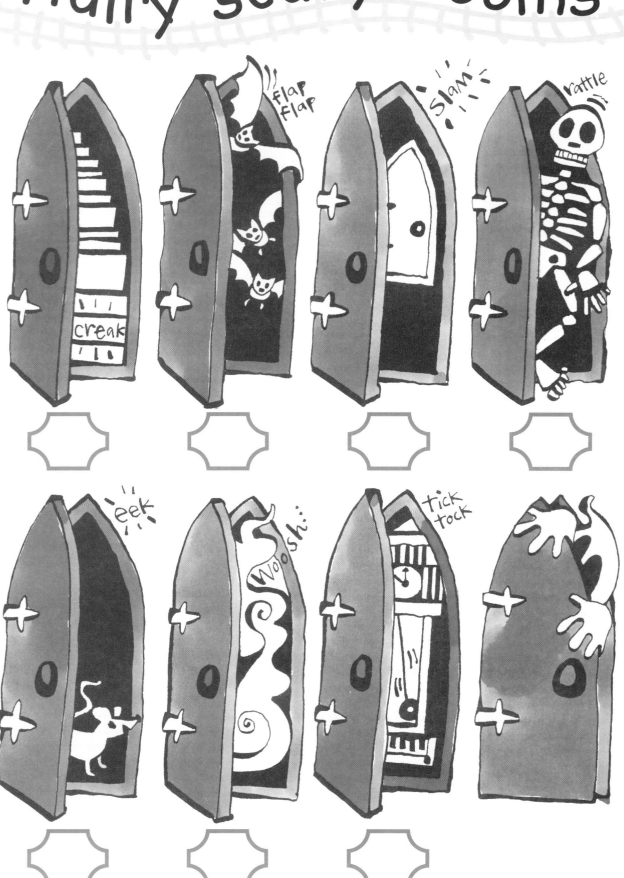

What's the score?
Exploring instruments and symbols

HAIRY SCARY

1 Learn The *Hairy Scary Castle* song

- Listen to The *Hairy Scary Castle* song, inviting the children to join in as it becomes familiar, then singing it again until it is quite secure:

In The Hairy Scary Castle,
In The Hairy Scary Castle,
In The Hairy Scary Castle,
Where the skeletons RATTLE,
And the ghosts go BOO!

In The Hairy Scary Castle ...
Where the rats go SQUEAK,
And the bats go FLAP!
And the skeletons RATTLE,
And the ghosts go BOO!

In The Hairy Scary Castle ...
Where the stairs go CREAK
And the clock goes TOCK!
Where the rats go SQUEAK,
And the bats go FLAP!
And the skeletons RATTLE,
And the ghosts go BOO!

In The Hairy Scary Castle ...
Where the wind goes WHOOSH,
And the doors go BANG!
Where the stairs go CREAK
And the clock goes TOCK!
Where the rats go SQUEAK,
And the bats go FLAP,
Where the skeletons RATTLE,
And the ghosts go BOO!

Teaching tip
- The order of the rooms is the hardest thing to remember in this song.

  It will help to make an enlarged set of cards from the *Hairy Scary rooms* photocopiable. Place these where everyone can see them in the order they appear in the song, and point to them as you sing the song.

2 Make actions, vocal and body sounds for *Hairy scary* rooms

- Remind the children of the castle rooms, referring them to an enlarged set of cards copied from the *Hairy scary rooms* photocopiable.

- As a class, choose actions, vocal and body sounds to represent each room, eg

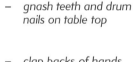

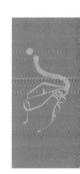

- gnash teeth and drum nails on table top

- clap backs of hands together

- make short, high vocal squeaks

- click tongues 'tick tock'

- make deep, creaky vocal sound

- stamp feet

- make whooshing mouth sounds

- Practise the sounds for each room in turn, 'opening' each room with a squeaky door vocal sound effect.

3 Play the *Hairy scary rooms* game with voices and actions

- Add the ghost room card to the set of seven room cards and shuffle them. Choose a child to be the dealer and eight other children to be the doors. The eight children stand in a row, with their backs to the class. The dealer stands behind the 'doors'.

The dealer turns over the first card in the shuffled pack and gives it to the first child in the row, who slowly turns to face the class, making a squeaky door sound, and revealing the card as they do so. The class respond with the matching sounds and actions prepared in activity 2.

The dealer turns over the next card, gives it to the next child, who turns, making the squeaky door sound, and revealing the card. Continue until all seven rooms have been 'opened' or until the ghost room card appears. The first child to call 'Boo' on seeing the ghost card becomes the next dealer.

Choose eight new room children. The new dealer shuffles the cards, and directs another journey through the haunted castle.

THE HAIRY SCARY CASTLE

1 **Compose *Hairy scary music* using instruments** p40

- Divide the class into seven groups, allocating one room from the castle to each. To remind them of their room, give each group the matching room card.

- Each group in turn selects their instruments from a wide variety of classroom percussion and sound-makers (*eg squeaky toys, blocks of wood, sandpaper, ridged plastic bottles, etc*).

- Give the groups time and space to rehearse the sounds for their room.

- Listen to each of the groups performing their room sounds. Direct the groups by holding up each card in turn while making the squeaky door sound. The listening children comment and offer suggestions for improvements.

2 **Notate scary room sounds** p43

- Give each group a large blank sheet of paper, and ask them to think of ways in which to notate their room music. They might use any of the ideas already explored in earlier lessons, eg

  - wooshing wind - pitch line with word 'shoooo' (see *Jamaquacks*)

  - ticking clock - illus of dots (see *Start conducting*)

  - squeaking mice - picture of mice

  - door bang - picture of a drum

- Each group in turn performs their room music from their score. The listening groups comment on how well the score represents the music. Are there improvements which can be made?

- Show the children The *Hairy Scary Castle* score. One room has ghosts inside, the others are blank. Invite a representative from each group to transfer the group's chosen notation onto the class score.

3 **Rehearse and perform *The Hairy Scary Castle***

- Appoint a conductor who will choose the route through the rooms of the Hairy Scary Castle. The conductor directs the seven groups by making the squeaky door sound, and pointing to the group's door. At any time in the route, the conductor may finish the music by opening the ghost's door, at which the whole class shouts, 'Boo!'

- Finally, perform the whole story (opposite). You narrate, everyone makes the squeaky door sound, the room groups make their sounds in the order presented in the story, and everyone sings the song.

- Record a performance, and give this to a younger class along with the *Hairy Scary Score* for them to enjoy at story time.

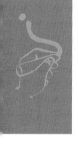

The Hairy Scary Castle

The Hairy Scary Castle is full of rooms ... and who knows what you might find in them! Slowly, you push open the door into the first room ... (Squeaky door) ... and it's full of rattling skeletons! (Skeleton group)

> In The Hairy Scary Castle,
> In The Hairy Scary Castle,
> In The Hairy Scary Castle,
>   Where the skeletons RATTLE,
>   And the ghosts go BOO!

You open the door to the second room ... (Squeaky door) ... and it's full of squeaking rats. (Rats group.)

You open the door to the third room ... (Squeaky door) ... and it's full of flapping bats! (Bats group.)

> In The Hairy Scary Castle ...
>   Where the rats go SQUEAK,
>   And the bats go FLAP!
>   And the skeletons RATTLE,
>   And the ghosts go BOO!

You open the door to the fourth room ... (Squeaky door) ... and you enter the shadowy hallway, with the big old grandfather clock ... (Clock group.)

You open the door to the fifth room ... (Squeaky door) ... and you're standing at the bottom of a dark flight of creaky stairs ... (Creaky stairs group.)

> In The Hairy Scary Castle ...
>   Where the stairs go CREAK
>   And the clock goes TOCK ...

You open the door to the sixth room ... (Squeaky door) ... and the wind goes whooshing through ... (Wind group.)

You open the door to the seventh room ... (Squeaky door) and all the doors behind you go BANG! (Doors group.)

> In The Hairy Scary Castle ...
>   Where the wind goes WHOOSH,
>   And the doors go BANG!
>   Where the stairs go CREAK
>   And the clock goes TOCK!
>   Where the rats go SQUEAK,
>   And the bats go FLAP,
>   Where the skeletons RATTLE,
>   And the ghosts go BOO!

Last of all, you open the door to the attic ... (Squeaky door) ... and the ghosts go: BOO!

Hairy Scary Castle

WHATEVER THE WEATHER

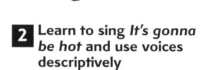

1 Listen to *Mahachagogo* and perform the chant in voices which describe different feelings 53

• Listen to the CD performance of the chant:

Leader:
Mahachagogo says:
Mmmmm,
Aaaaah,
Oooh,
Lah lah lah,
Then he stops.
Why?
Nor do I.
But I do know that when he feels cold –

Children:
Mmmmm,
Aaaaah,
Oooh,
Lah lah lah,
Then he stops.
I don't know.

Mahachagogo says *(as though feeling cold)*:
Mmmmm,
Aaaaah,
Oooh,
Lah lah lah,
Then he stops.
Why?
Nor do I.
But I do know that when he feels hot –

Mmmmm,
Aaaaah,
Oooh,
Lah lah lah,
Then he stops.
I don't know.

Mahachagogo says *(as though feeling hot)*:
Mmmmm,
Aaaaah,
Oooh,
Lah lah lah,
Then he stops.
Why?
Nor do I.
But I do know that when he feels tired –

Mmmmm,
Aaaaah,
Oooh,
Lah lah lah,
Then he stops.
I don't know.

Mahachagogo says no more.

• Ask the children to describe how the voices changed when Mahachagogo was feeling cold. *(Shivery, freezing, wobbly, high-pitched, shorter.)* Ask how the voices changed when Mahachagogo was feeling hot? *(Slower, lower, longer, smoother.)*

• Perform the chant as a class. You lead, the children follow. Encourage the children to find their own ways of making their voices sound cold then hot.

2 Learn to sing *It's gonna be hot* and use voices descriptively 54-55

• Teach the song, using track 54.

Vs 1 It's gonna be hot, hot, hot, hot,
That's what the weatherlady said.
It's gonna be hot, hot, hot, hot,
That's what the weatherman said.
It's time for the
T shirts, T shirts,
Beach ball, beach ball
Paddling pool, paddling pool,
Sun! Sun! Sun!
It's gonna be hot ...

Vs 2 It's gonna be wet, wet, wet, wet ...
It's time for the
Raincoat, raincoat,
Wellies, wellies,
Wet play, wet play,
Rain! Rain! Rain!
It's gonna be wet, wet, wet, wet ...

• Ask the children to suggest ways of using their voices to describe the weather in each verse *(eg making the word 'hot' long, smooth, and breathy; making the word 'wet' short and sharp)*.

• All perform the song to backing track 55, using voices descriptively.

3 Listen to *Light showers, sunny spells* to identify and describe the sounds 56

• Explain to the children that they will hear a piece of music which describes weather. Ask them to identify the weather. *(Rain showers followed by sunshine.)*

• Ask the children to describe the sounds that they heard. *(Splashing, dripping, pouring, drying, shining, heat.)*

RAIN AND SUN FUN

1 Learn to sing *Majā pade* 57-58))

- Teach the song, using track 57:

Vs1   Rainfall, rainfall, dripping and splashing,
Rainfall, rainfall, dripping and splashing,
Let's all be happy, splashing in the falling rain.
Let's all be happy, splashing in the falling rain.

Varasād, varasād, sarsar varaso,
Varasād, varasād, sarsar varaso,
Majā pade amane – bhijavāni,
Majā pade amane – bhijavāni,

Vs2   Sun shine, sun shine, sun shine in splendour ...
Let's all be happy wandering in the sunshine ...

Sooraj sooraj chamko chamko ...
Majā pade amane – faravāni ...

- Perform the song with the English or Gujerati lyrics to track 58.

2 Select instruments to accompany *Majā pade* 58))

- Ask the children to suggest instruments which might accompany each of the verses to describe the rain fall and the sun shine, eg

  – sun: cymbals and soft beaters, triangles, tambourines shaken gently;

  – rain: woodblocks, castanets, claves, rainsticks

- Select a small group of children to accompany the first verse. Give these children the chosen instruments. As the class sing the first verse, the players add their sounds freely in the background.

- Select a second group to accompany the second verse. Practise adding these sounds as the class sing.

- Perform the whole song to track 58, adding instrumental accompaniments.

- Repeat with different playing groups.

Teaching tip

- As they listen to **It's gonna be hot** and **Maja pade** ask the children to notice when words or lines are repeated. To help them learn the songs, ask them to listen first and then join in with each repeat.

3 Listen to *Majā pade* to notice and identify the accompanying instruments 59))

- All listen to the performance of *Majā pade* on track 59. Ask the children to notice the instruments they hear in the accompaniment to each verse and to remember when they have heard these sounds before (*Lesson 1 activity 3*).

  As a class, identify and name the instruments.

- Ask why they think these instruments might have been chosen, eg

  – because the cymbal makes a long, shining, warm sound;

  – the woodblock sounds like short, drips of rain.

- Compare the two performances of *Majā pade* – the children's own (activity 2), and the one on track 59:

  – were any of the sounds the class chose similar or played on the same instruments?

  – were the instruments played differently or in the same way?

Teaching tip

- Encourage the children playing instruments to listen to each other and to the singers to make sure that the sounds do not drown the voices.

CLOUDS GATHERING

1 Listen to *Storm* and describe the effect

- All listen to the CD, joining in with the repeated line 'splish splash splish splash', and matching the changing volume:

1 Hush_____ Hush_____
Splish splash splish splash

2 Rush dash rush dash
Splish splash splish splash

3 Slish slosh slish slosh
Splish splash splish splash

4 Bash lash bash lash
Splish splash splish splash

All CRASH____ FLASH____
Splish splash splish splash

4 Bash lash bash lash
Splish splash splish splash

3 Slish slosh slish slosh
Splish splash splish splash

2 Rush dash rush dash
Splish splash splish splash

1 Hush_____ Hush_____
Splish splash splish splash

All Wishhhhhhhhhhhhhhhhhhhhh_____

- Ask the children what the chant describes. (*A rainstorm.*)

- How does the chant describe the progress of a storm? (*It starts quietly as the rain begins to fall, and becomes louder and louder, gradually dying away after the thunder and lightning.*)

- As a class, consider how the effect of a storm is achieved, eg

  – *what is being described by each pair of words, eg 'rush dash' (people running to get under cover)*

  – *how do individual words add to the effect?*

  – *how does the voice change? (It gets louder then quieter.)*

2 Perform *Storm* and control the volume

- All listen to track 61 and notice how the storm effect is achieved this time. (*An extra voice is added in each pair of lines then taken away.*)

- Write the chant on the board, numbering the pairs of lines. Divide into four groups, one for each pair of lines.

- Perform the chant in the arrangement given in track 60 (*you conduct by pointing to each pair of lines as they are said*):

  – each group in turn says their pair of lines – group 1 chants very quietly, group 2 a little louder, and so on;

  – all say the middle pair of lines and the last line;

- As a class, consider the effectiveness of the performance:

  – did the chanting increase in volume from one group to the next during the first part (*crescendo*), and did it decrease in volume from one group to the next in the second part (*diminuendo*)?

  If necessary, perform the chant again with an improved crescendo and diminuendo.

- Now perform the chant in the track 61 arrangement.

  – group 1 begins and continues – at the same volume – to the written repeat of their lines;

  – group 2 joins in and continues – at the same volume – until the written repeat of their lines, and so on.

  – all interrupt their lines to say the middle and last lines.

- As a class, consider the effectiveness of the performance:

  – did the chant increase then decrease in volume effectively as each group joined in and dropped out?

  – were the words clear, or did all the extra voices make them difficult to hear? Can this be improved with practice?

3 Perform *Storm* with instruments and control volume

- In the groups from activity 2, the children select instruments which best match the volume of the four pairs of lines, eg 1: 'hush hush' – egg shakers, 2: 'rush dash' – maraca, etc.

- As a class, check that the chosen instruments provide an effective crescendo by listening to each group's words and sounds one by one. If not, consider how this can be achieved, eg each group plays louder, or chooses another instrument which makes a louder sound.

- Perform the chant in the track 60 arrangement, each group chanting and playing in turn. All chant and play the middle and last lines. Consider the effectiveness of the crescendo and diminuendo achieved, and improve if necessary. Record a performance.

- Perform the chant in the track 61 arrangement with the groups joining in and dropping out cumulatively, then record the performance.

  All listen to the two recordings and compare them

  – was either more exciting?

  – more effective?

  – clearer?

BUILDERS AT WORK

1 **Sing *Gonna build a house boat* with actions**

- Listen to the CD together then teach the song:

  Gonna build a house boat, gonna build it fine,
  Gonna build it right, so I hammer in time.
  　Tap tap tap tap goes the hammer,
  　Tap tap tap tap goes the hammer,
  　Tap tap tap tap goes the hammer,
  Oh Noah, gonna build it fine.

  Gonna build a house boat, gonna build it fine,
  Gonna build it right, so I saw in time.
  　Zzz zzz zzz zzz goes the woodsaw ...

  Gonna build a house boat, gonna build it fine,
  Gonna build it right, so I chisel in time,
  　Chip chip chip chip goes the chisel ...

  Gonna build a house boat, gonna build it fine,
  Gonna build it right, so I paint in time,
  　Wish wash wish wash goes the paintbrush ...

- All sing the song to backing track 63, making building actions on the beat from the action section to the end of each verse:

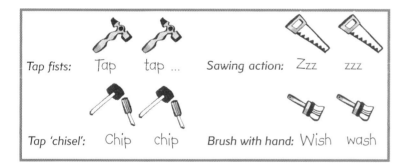

2 **Select and layer sounds for an accompaniment to *Gonna build a house boat***

- Divide the class into four groups, one for each verse of *Gonna build a house boat*. Give each group the appropriate card from the *Builder's yard* photocopiable.

  In their groups, the children discuss which instruments might represent their building scene, eg hammering – woodblocks.

- Each group nominates two or three children to play the instruments they have chosen.

  Rehearse each group's verse. The singers begin and the players join at the action section, playing on the beat through to the end of the verse.

- Perform the song to the backing track, noting the eight cowbell beats which introduce the backing track and are repeated between each verse. Perform again, swapping singers and players.

- Perform the song again without the backing track. You lead the performance by tapping the beat on a cowbell:

Explain to the children that the tempo will change during the performance, so everyone must listen carefully. Begin the performance, and gradually increase the speed of the cowbell beat (*you might get gradually faster to the end of the third verse, and slow down during the last verse*). Did everyone listen well and keep in time?

3 **Improvise a performance of *Builder's yard***

- The aim is for the four groups from activity 2 to create a piece of instrumental music called *Builder's yard*.

  This time the groups improvise their sounds. They play freely, each observing their own tempo, sometimes fast, sometimes slow, pausing to rest occasionally. Give each group practise in playing their sounds.

- The conductor leads a performance by pointing to any of the *Builder's yard* pictures in any order. The groups play only when their card is indicated.

- Appoint two conductors and improvise another performance, following the two conductors' signals. Discuss what happened this time. (*Sometimes two groups were playing at the same time, sometimes the conductors both pointed to the same card.*)

- Repeat with another two conductors. Ask the groups to listen carefully to the effects they are producing, paying particular attention to the various combinations of sounds, eg noticing which groups played together, and which combinations worked well.

Builder's yard

Tap tap tap tap goes the hammer

Zzz zzz zzz zzz goes the wood saw

Chip chip chip chip goes the chisel

Wish wash wish wash goes the paintbrush

FLOOD WARNING

1 Add sounds to the recording of *Noah's ark*

* Ask the children, as they listen to the recording of *Noah's ark*, to think of what sounds might follow the line 'And it sounded just like this'. Encourage them to consider vocal sounds and body percussion. Play the CD again, and all improvise the sound ideas.

* Discuss the improvised sounds, and all decide which were effective, and which might be improved to capture the mood of each verse:

  – busy builders, noisy excited animals, the misery of the rain, fear of the storm, boredom drifting at sea, hope of the dove's return. *(Use the ideas in the Teaching tips box if necessary.)*

* Play the CD again and record the children adding their chosen sounds. *(Use a video camera if one is available.)*

Teaching tips

* Note the signal at the end of each instrumental interlude which tells the children that the next verse is about to start.
* Encourage the children to draw on the experiences of previous lessons, eg
  – the use of vocal timbre (sound quality) for expression in Lesson 1; the careful selection of instrumental timbre in Lessons 2, 3 and 4.
  – the use of dynamics/volume to create storm effects in Lesson 3.
  – the use of tempo to convey urgent work in Lesson 4.

2 Sing *Noah's ark* and play *Storyteller* to recognise the episodes of the story p50

* Show the children the six cards from the *Noah's ark* photocopiable and together put them in the order of the story where they can be seen by everyone. Teach the song, pointing to the cards to remind the children of the order of the first six verses.

* Choose a child to be the storychanger who will change the order of the story. Give this child the set of *Noah's ark* cards. The storychanger shuffles the cards and holds up the first one. The class respond by singing the appropriate verse. Continue until all the cards have been shown and placed in the muddled order.

* Now choose a child to be the storyteller who will put the story in the correct order. This child reorders the cards and holds them up one at a time while the others respond. Is the story back in the correct order? If not, who can put it right? When the story is correct, all sing the closing verse, ending with a loud, 'Hooray'.

3 Perform *Noah's ark* without the CD

* Explain that the children are going to perform *Noah's ark* without the CD. They will sing the song themselves and perform vocal and body percussion sounds after each verse. Ask them if they would like to change anything now that there is no backing track, eg

  – *the speed and volume of the verses may be changed from one verse to the next;*

  – *the interludes may be longer, freer, or structured differently.*

* Rehearse the new arrangement, inviting further appraisal. Record a final performance.

Noah's ark

Noah built an ark,
He went and built an ark,
He took a saw and hammer
And he went and built an ark.
    And it sounded just like this!
    interlude

They came in two by two,
They came in two by two,
God sent the animals,
They came in two by two.
    And it sounded just like this!
    interlude

The rain began to fall,
The rain began to fall,
The waters were a-rising
As the rain began to fall.
    And it sounded just like this!
    interlude

The waves were very high,
The waves were very high,
The ark kept a-floating,
Tho' the waves were very high.
    And it sounded just like this!
    interlude

They drifted on the sea,
They drifted on the sea,
All around was water
As they drifted on the sea.
    And it sounded just like this!
    interlude

Noah sent a dove,
A raven, then a dove,
She brought him back an olive branch,
Noah sent a dove.
    And she sounded just like this!
    interlude

Noah's safe at last,
Noah's safe at last,
He's safely back on land again
Noah's safe at last!
    And it sounded just like this!
    HOORAY!

Noah's ark cards

Noah built an ark

They came in two by two

The rain began to fall

The waves were very high

They drifted on the sea

Noah sent a dove

NOAH'S ARK

1 Perform Noah's ark with instrumental interludes

- Remind the children of the song and sing it together.

- Discuss the instruments the children would use after each verse to represent 'And it sounded just like this'. Let individuals demonstrate their ideas.

- Divide into six groups, allocating the story episodes by giving each group one of the *Noah's ark* cards. Distribute the chosen instruments. Give each group time and space to listen to the CD and to practise making the sounds for their episode.

- Rehearse the song all the way through with the groups performing their compositions after each verse. Remind the children to listen for the signal which tells them to stop playing before the next verse.

- Record a final performance, and video it if possible.

2 Retell the *Noah's ark* story with instruments

- Position the *Noah's ark* cards where everyone can see them.

  Explain that the children are going to retell the story using instruments alone – without singing or using track 64.

  The lack of backing track offers the groups freedom to extend or restructure their piece, using ideas developed in Lesson 5 activity 3.

  Encourage each group to consider how best to make a clear beginning and ending, eg

  – *one player starts then the rest of the group join in one by one, and drop out in reverse order;*

  – *appoint a conductor to signal start and stop.*

    (*The groups will need to choose the method most appropriate for their episode of the story.*)

- The groups listen to each piece to familiarise themselves with each other's chosen structure and ending, then rehearse playing the episodes one after another in the order of the story. Appraise the result, eg

  – *were the endings clear?*

  – *did the groups come in on time, making a seamless story in sound.*

- Record a final performance.

3 Appraise the recordings of *Noah's ark* and share them with another class

- Listen to the four recordings from Lesson 5 activities 1 and 3, and from Lesson 6 activities 1 and 2. Ask the children to say what they like best about each, and to describe how they differ. Do they think the version without words tells the story as clearly as the others?

- Give the recordings to another class. Ask them to listen and discuss what they liked best about each version of the story. Compare their reactions with yours. Did they notice anything different?

SOUND STARTERS

1 **Play *Sunrise sounds* to identify sounds in the environment** p53 65-66))

- Show the class the cards from the *Sunrise sounds* photocopiable. Listen to track 65 together (ordered 1–6). Ask the children to identify each of the early morning sounds and match them to the picture cards.

  Discuss the detail of each set of sounds, noticing how well they match the detail in the cards.

- Ask individual children to make the sounds for each card using their voices or bodies. Did the others think the sounds were a good match? Improve if necessary, and all copy.

- Now play track 66 (ordered 421365). Afterwards invite a volunteer to reorder the cards to match the track, and direct the class to make the rehearsed vocal or body sounds for each card in turn. Was the order correct? Listen to the CD to check, and continue ordering as necessary.

Teaching tip

- Encourage a child who has difficulty focusing their listening to pick one thing from the photocopiable and listen for its sound.

Background information

Sun arise is accompanied by the didgeridoo, an Australian aboriginal instrument. It is a piece of wood hollowed out by termites and then decorated with traditional aboriginal symbols.

2 **Listen and move to *Sun arise*** 67))

- As they listen to the CD, lead the children in the actions suggested, either standing in a large ring, or moving freely about a large open space. Encourage large, free, expressive movements:

  – first section: on 'sun arise' spread arms in an arc; on 'fluttering', 'spreading', 'glistening', 'lighting up' gesture to left and right with hands and arms

  – second section: stamp on the strong beats in the music; make a pushing motion with hands and arms as if 'driving away the darkness'.

3 **Play the *Post calypso* game to make a variety of sounds using voices** p53 68))

- Use the CD to teach the song:

  Here comes the postie,
  Out very early,
  Up with the bright sun,
  Off on the post run,
  Rat tat tat tat tat,
  Card on the doormat,
  Sounds like they're having fun.

Teaching tip

- Teach the song by echo-singing it: you sing a line and the children copy, sing the next line and so on.

- Look at the three enlarged cards from the *Postcards* photocopiable. Ask individuals to suggest vocal sounds for each of the pictures, then all copy the suggested sounds (*eg* plane - brrrrrrr whoooosh).

- Cut out three blank postcards. Take suggestions for three more pictures and invite volunteers to draw them. Decide together on sounds for each new picture (*eg* seagull - ark ark ark).

- Now place the postcards in a cloth bag and choose a postie to move amongst the children as you all sing the song. At the song's end the postie offers the bag to the nearest child. This child takes out a postcard and makes the vocal sound to match the picture. The others say which card it matches and all copy the sound made. Continue the game with a new postie.

Sunrise sounds

1

2

3

4

5

6

Postcards

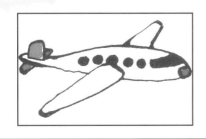

SOUND SORTERS

1 Sing *Just a load of rubbish* to explore junk instruments **69**

- Listen to the CD together and ask the children what junk instrument is being played (*rice pot shaker*):

Vs   Feel around in my big box
       Take your time_____ (*pause*)
       What have you got?

Ch   Just a load af rubbish but it makes a lovely sound
       Shake it high, shake it low, shake it all around.

- Teach the song then play the game:

  - place a selection of junk soundmakers in a large open box (shake: *pots of beads, pasta, buttons, milk bottle tops, sand*; tap: *stout cardboard boxes and tins with a selection of sticks and brushes for beaters*; scrape: *corrugated card and pencils*); place the three cards face down beside the box;

  - as you sing the verse, a volunteer comes out, turns up one of the cards and selects an instrument to play;

  - as everyone sings the chorus (*altering 'shake' to 'tap' or 'scrape'*) the child plays freely.

Photocopiable shake, tap and scrape cards to enlarge

2 Play the *Just junk* game p55

- This is a game for any number of players and a leader. Make the pictured soundmakers available and let the children try out their sounds. Give each child a copy of the *Just junk* photocopiable. The instruments are numbered 1–4. The players use the blank strips to record the order in which the instruments are played by the leader.

  The leader takes the instruments behind a screen, and writes on the first strip the order in which they will be played, eg

  1 4 3 2

  The leader plays accordingly and the listeners write the order on the first strip of their photocopiable.

  The leader repeats the game until all four strips have been used. The screen is removed and the leader repeats each sound sequence while the listeners check their results.

- The children can find a new set of four soundmakers, number them and draw them on the *Just your junk* photocopiable, then play again.

3 Play the *Post calypso* game with junk instruments p53 **68**

- Using the box of soundmakers from activity 1, play the *Post calypso* game again. Choose a postie to move amongst the children as you all sing. At the end of the song the child who selects a postcard chooses a soundmaker which they think will match the picture on the card, eg

  - dog: *sandpaper scraper*;

  - car: *metal washers rattled together*;

  - horse: *yoghurt pots tapped together*.

- Repeat the game several times, asking the class to evaluate the effectiveness of the sounds and suggest improvements.

Teaching tips

- To begin with, remove the screen and check the answers after each turn.

- Play the game as a class, then in small groups in the music corner.

Just junk

1st			

2nd			

3rd			

4th			

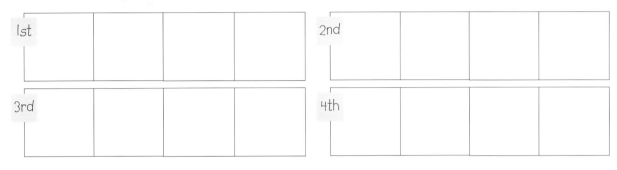

Just your junk

1st			

2nd			

3rd			

4th			

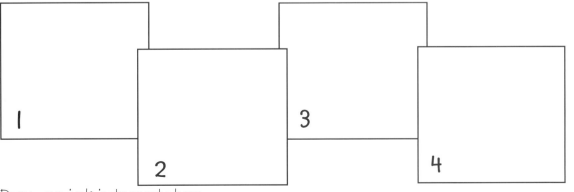

Draw your junk instruments here

Music Express Year 2 © A & C Black 2002
www.acblack.com/musicexpress

3rd Sounds interesting
Exploring sounds

SALLY GO ROUND THE SUN

1 Sing *Sally go round the sun* and tap the beat and the rhythm on body percussion

- Explain that *Sally go round the sun* is the type of song which might be used in a pre-school. The song will form part of a final performance which describes a day in the life of Sally, who attends pre-school. All listen to the CD. The song is sung then repeated on instruments. Teach the song like this:

    – sing along with the CD, tapping the beat on your knees and all shouting 'hoi!';

    – tap the rhythm of the words with fingers on palms during the instrumental repeat.

    Sally go round the sun,
    Sally go round the moon,
    Sally go round the chimney pots
    On a Monday afternoon, Hoi!

- Sing along to the CD again. During the instrumental repeat, all tap along with the rhythm of the melody using any body percussion, eg slice palms, tap shoulders or chest, tap cheek, brush knees.

2 Sing *Sally go round the sun* and tap the beat and rhythm on instruments

- Give everyone a small home-made shaker.

    Sing the song with or without the CD. During the sung verse, sing the words and tap the beat on the shakers. Tap the rhythm of the words during the instrumental verse.

- Choose one child (*or more if there is space*) to walk to the beat of the sung verse, and dances on the spot to the instrumental verse, while everyone else sings and plays.

3 Rehearse different arrangements of *Sally go round the sun*

- Invite the children to choose instruments from the selection of soundmakers used in previous lessons and place them on the floor ready to play. Perform the song without the CD like this:

    – first time: whisper the words while quietly tapping the beat with fingers on palms, then sing the song in your heads while tapping the rhythm of the words;

    – second time: sing in normal voices while tapping the beat quietly on knees, then sing the song in your heads while performing the rhythm of the words using a wide variety of body percussion;

    – third time: pick up the soundmakers and play the beat as you sing the song, then sing the song in your heads while playing the rhythm of the words;

    – fourth time: sing slowly and tiredly, as though at the end of a long day then improvise yawns while tapping the rhythm of the words on body percussion.

TEATIME SOUNDMAKERS

1 **Sing *Teatime shout* with tap, scrape, shake actions**

- Use the CD to teach the song. Join in with the chorus as it becomes familiar. Add the playing actions indicated by the words as you sing the verses:

Ch   Let's make a meal for a hungry little sister,
      Let's make a meal for a hungry little girl.
      What shall we make for a hungry little sister?
      What shall we make for a hungry little girl?

Vs1   Oh, tap on the saucepan lid and shout,
        curry for me, curry for you,
      Oh, tap on the saucepan lid and shout,
        curry for me and you.

Ch   Let's make a meal for a hungry little sister ...

Vs2   Oh, scrape a potato skin and shout,
        chips for me, chips for you ...

Ch   Let's make a meal for a hungry little sister ...

Vs3   Oh, shake up a pan of maize and shout,
        popcorn for me, popcorn for you ...

3 **Accompany *Teatime shout* with kitchen soundmakers**

- Make available the selection of soundmakers used in previous lessons supplemented with kitchen soundmakers, eg:

  – *ladles, saucepans and lids, chopsticks, plastic bottle half-filled with water, wooden spoons, cheese grater ...*

  Invite volunteers to demonstrate tapping, scraping and shaking sounds on the new instruments (*eg tap saucepan or scrape cheese grater with wooden spoon, shake maize in a jar*).

- Remind the children of the three favourite tapping, scraping and shaking verses from *Teatime shout* and discuss the soundmakers the children would choose to accompany each verse.

- Divide into three groups – one per verse – and allocate the chosen soundmakers. Choose a child from each group to be the group's cook. The cook may sing the chorus as a solo. The class sing the answer, while the cook leads his or her group playing the beat and/or the rhythm of the words on the chosen soundmakers:

  Cook sings: Let's make a meal ...

  All sing: Oh, tap on the saucepan lid ...

  accompanied by cook's group playing soundmakers.

2 **Make up new verses for *Teatime shout***

- Invite ideas for other meals to make, encouraging the children to think of the actions which might accompany the preparation (*chopping, slicing, mashing, whipping, tossing, frying, boiling*).

- Sing the new verses the children have suggested, eg

  Mix up some egg and flour
     and shout,
       cake for me, cake for you ...

- As a class discuss whether the sounds for each verse would fall into the category of scraping, tapping or shaking.

  Decide on three favourite verses from the existing and new ones, which represent tapping, shaking and scraping sounds respectively. Draw a set of symbols to remind you of their order (*eg popcorn pan, potato, saucepan*).

Teaching tip
- Pair children who are less confident about singing solo with a more confident child.

SUNSET SOUNDS

1 Listen to *When I go to bed* to identify sounds in the environment

- Ask the children what kind of sounds they are used to hearing outdoors and inside their home, as they wait to go to sleep.

- All listen to track 72 with eyes closed, imagining that, like the child in the song, you are lying in bed and listening to evening sounds. (*The track gives the first verse of the song, followed by the evening sounds the child hears.*)

- On a second listening, make a class list of the sounds everyone heard (the answers are given in the song lyrics below – track 73).

Vs1   When I go to bed I lie as quiet as a mouse,
        And listen to the friendly noises drifting round the house.

Vs2   The far-off sound of talking and the creaking of the floor,
        Music from the radio, the banging of a door.

Vs3   The sound of people's footsteps as they walk along the street,
        Clicks and creaks and rumbles as the radiators heat.

Vs4   Cups and saucers clinking as they're washed and put to dry.
        Barking dogs and yowling cats, the buzzing of a fly.

Vs5   The rumbling sound of traffic and a sudden noisy laugh,
        Splashing from the bathroom as my sister has a bath.

- Teach the song, using track 73.

2 Rehearse sounds to accompany *When I go to bed*

- Discuss the sound sources the children might use to make the evening sounds in the song. Make available the full range of soundmakers used in earlier lessons, and encourage the children to think of vocal and body percussion sounds as well. Annotate the class list of evening sounds from activity 1 with the children's soundmaker suggestions.

- Divide the class into four groups – one each for verses 2 to 5. Allocate the chosen soundmakers to each group and ask the children to rehearse the sounds which follow their verse. These may be rhythmic or free. Give each group time and space to practise the sounds with track 74 (*interlude backing track*).

- Each group in turn performs their evening sounds to track 74, while the others listen and assess their effectiveness. Ask the listeners to say what they thought was effective, and what could be improved. Invite the groups to perform again, using the suggestions for improvement.

3 Perform sound interludes between the verses of *When I go to bed*

- Play track 75 and sing the song, noting that the interludes between the verses do not include the evening sounds.

- In the four groups from activity 2, rehearse a performance of the song, adding the rehearsed evening sounds to the interludes after each verse like this:

yeowl...

Verse 1	Verse 2	talking creaking floor radio banging door	Verse 3	footsteps radiators	Verse 4	cups and saucers dogs cats fly	Verse 5	traffic laughter bathtime

SALLY'S DAY

1 **Rehearse tapping, shaking and scraping accompaniments to three songs**

- Divide into three groups – shakers, scrapers and tappers – and allocate a collection of soundmakers to each. Rehearse the songs and accompaniments to:

  - *Post calypso*: each group selects a card to represent with their soundmakers, then all sing the song followed by each group's sounds;

  - *Just a load of rubbish*: place a shaking, a tapping and a scraping soundmaker in the box, and invite a volunteer to select one during the singing of the verse. This child then leads the appropriate group playing an accompaniment as everyone sings the chorus. Continue with two more volunteers.

  - *Teatime treats*: practise playing the accompaniments to the three favourite verses devised in Lesson 4 activity 3.

2 **Rehearse movement and dance for *Sun arise***

- As a class, revise the movement and dance work for *Sun arise*, Lesson 1 activity 2. All move to the music, remembering the two sections and the movements devised for them.

- Invite a small group of volunteers to perform the *Sun arise* dance, moving around all the available space, while the others watch and contribute ideas for improving the dance.

3 **Direct a performance of *From sunrise to sunset***

- Show the *From sunrise to sunset* photocopiable to the class (a single page version of the score is given on the CD-ROM). Explain that it shows a day in the life of a little girl called Sally.

- Discuss each stage of the day shown on the score, and notice the activities which each picture represents. Divide into the groups from activity 1, then rehearse the cycle in this order:

 – *Sun arise* (*track 67*): the movement group perform their dance;

 – *Sally go round the sun* (*waking Sally up*): all whisper the words, then tap the word rhythms quietly on palms;

 – *Postman's knocking*: as rehearsed above;

 – *Sally go round the sun* (*Sally going to pre-school*): all sing and tap the beat then play the word rhythms on body percussion;

 – *Just a load of rubbish* (*Sally playing at pre-school*): as rehearsed above;

 – *Sally go round the sun* (*Sally going home*): all sing and tap the beat then play word rhythms on soundmakers;

 – *Teatime treats* (*Sally's evening meal*): as rehearsed above;

 – *Sally go round the sun* (*Sally's bedtime*): all sing and tap the beat then play word rhythms on body percussion slowly and tiredly

 – *When I go to bed* (*track 73*): all listen with eyes closed;

 – *Sally go round the sun* (*singing Sally to sleep*): all whisper the words and tap the beat then quietly tap the word rhythms.

- Perform *From sunrise to sunset* during an assembly on PHSE. (*Change 'Monday' in Sally go round the sun to the appropriate day of the week.*)

From sunrise

to sunset

Index

Index of songs, stories and chants (titles and *first lines*)

Videoclips

There are 17 videoclips for teachers (see introduction notes p6)

Audio CD track list

Track Contents CD 1

The long and short of it

1 *Some sounds are short* with card 3 sounds (page 8, 10)
2 *Dipidu* (8, 10)
3 *Jackass wid him long tail* (8, 10)
4 *Dipidu* clapped beat (10)
5 *Dipidu* cymbal playing the beat (10)
6 *Dipidu* clapped word rhythms (10)
7 *Dipidu* claves playing word rhythms (10)
8 *Dipidu* backing track (10)
9 *Jackass wid him long tail* with scraper accompaniment (10)
10 *Tinga layo* (11)
11 *Tinga layo* word rhythms (11)
12 *Tinga layo* new words rhythms (13)
13 *Tinga layo* with word rhythm accompaniments (13)
14 *Tinga layo* backing track (13)
15 *Mi caballo blanco* (13, 14, 15)
16 *The jockeys' dance* (14)
17 *Mi caballo blanco* drum pattern (14)
18 *Mi caballo blanco* teaching track (14, 15)

Feel the pulse

19 *Down the avenue* (16)
20 *March past of the kitchen utensils* (16, 18)
21 *Kye kye kule* (16)
22 *Someone's in the kitchen with Dinah* (18, 19)
23 *Kye kye kule* beat (18, 19)
24 *Kye kye kule* rhythm (18, 19)
25 *Someone's in the kitchen with Dinah* with tambourine (19)
26 *Someone's in the kitchen with Dinah* backing track (19)
27 *What's the time Mr Wolf?* (19)
28 *What's the time Mr Wolf?* - clapping answers (19)
29 *A plate of potatoes* (21, 22)
30 *How many people here for dinner?* (22, 23)
31 *How many people here for dinner?* - layering one rhythm (22)
32 *How many people here for dinner* layering three rhythms (22, 23)
33 *Chinese kitchen* (22)

Taking off

34 *I jump out of bed in the morning* first verse (24)
35 *I jump out of bed* all verses (24)
36 *Looby Loo* (24, 26)
37 *Six little ducks that I once knew* (24, 26)

38 *Jazzyquacks* (26)
39 *The prehistoric animal brigade* (28, 32, 33)
40 *The prehistoric animal brigade* first verse (28)
41 *Fossils* melody on xylophone and piano (28)
42 *Fossils* (28, 33)
43 *Prehistoric animal brigade* with drone accompaniment (29, 33)
44 *Fossils in the rock* (29, 32, 33)
45 *Fossils in the rock* with drone accompaniment (29)

What's the score?

46 *Make your sounds like mine* (34)
47 *Sound puzzle* (34)
48 *Sextet* (34)
49 *Start conducting* (35)
50 *Cartoon strip* (37, 39)
51 *Hairy scary sounds* (39)
52 *Hairy Scary Castle song* (41)

Rain rain go away

53 *Mahachagogo* (44)
54 *It's gonna be hot* (44)
55 *It's gonna be hot* backing track (44)
56 *Light showers sunny spells* (44)
57 *Majā pade* (45)
58 *Majā pade* backing track (45)
59 *Majā pade* with *Light showers sunny spells* backing (45)
60 *Storm* (46)
61 *Storm* with layered voices (46)
62 *Gonna build a house boat* (47)
63 *Gonna build a house boat* backing track (47)
64 *Noah's ark* (49, 51)

Sounds interesting

65 *Sunrise sounds* - (52)
66 *Sunrise sounds* - (52)
67 *Sun arise* (52, 59)
68 *Post calypso* (52, 54)
69 *Just a load of rubbish* (54)
70 *Sally go round the sun* (56)
71 *Teatime shout* (57)
72 *When I go to bed* first verse and evening sounds interludes (58)
73 *When I go to bed* song (58, 59)
74 *When I go to bed* interlude backing (58)
75 *When I go to bed* song and interlude backings (58)

Acknowledgements

The author and publishers would like to thank all the teachers and consultants who assisted in the preparation of this series: Meriel Ascott, Francesca Bedford, Chris Bryant, Yolanda Cattle, Stephen Chadwick, Veronica Clark, Tania Demidova, Veronica Hanke, Maureen Hanke, Emily Haward, Jocelyn Lucas, Carla Moss, Danny Monte, Lio Moscardini, Sue Nicholls, Vanessa Olney, Mrs S Pennington, Pauline Quinton, Ana Sanderson, Jane Sebba, Heather Scott, Michelle Simpson, Debbie Townsend and Joy Woodall.

Helen Chadwick, Kevin Graal, Missak Takoushian and Stephen, Alex and Aidan Chadwick performed the songs and chants recorded for the CD. Thanks are also due to all who performed for previous recordings for A&C Black publications which have been reused in *Music Express Year 2*.

Helen MacGregor and Year 3 children of Brunswick Park Primary School performed the activities demonstrated on the CD-ROM videoclips.

The following copyright material has been created for *Music Express* by A&C Black or is previously published in A&C Black publications:

A plate of potatoes by Kaye Umansky and **Storm** by Helen MacGregor from *Bingo lingo*, published by A&C Black © 1999.

Make your sound like mine and **Some sounds are short**, words by Sue Nicholls from *Bobby Shaftoe, clap your hands*, published by A&C Black, © 1992.

Just a load of rubbish and **When I go to bed** , words and music by Veronica Clark, from *High Low Dolly Pepper*, published by A&C Black, © 1991.

Fossils in the rock by Helen MacGregor from *Listening to Music 5+*, published by A&C Black © 1995.

Down the avenue and **Sound puzzle** words by Sue Nicholls from *Michael Finnigin, tap your chinigin*, published by A&C Black, © 1998.

Mahachagogo by Ana Sanderson © 1997, from *Songbirds: ME*, published by A&C Black.

It's gonna be hot by Jane Sebba © 1997 from *Songbirds: SEASONS*, published by A & C Black.

The Hairy Scary Castle and **Noah's ark** from *Three Singing Pigs* by Kaye Umansky, published by A&C Black, © 1994

Cartoon strip, Hairy scary sounds, Jazzyquacks, Light showers sunny spells, and **Sunrise sounds** by Stephen Chadwick created for *Music Express*, © 2002

Start conducting (words), **Looby Loo** (verses 2 and 3) and arrangement of **What's the time Mr Wolf** by Helen MacGregor created for *Music Express*, © 2002

How many people here for dinner? Post calypso (words), **Teatime shout** (words) by Sheena Roberts created for *Music Express*, © 2002

Jackass wid him long tail and **Tinga layo** from *Mango spice*; **I jump out of bed in the morning, Six little ducks** and **Someone's in the kitchen with Dinah** from *Okki-tokki-unga*; **Kye kye kule** from *Songbirds: ME*; **Dipidu** from *Tinderbox*; **Sally go round the sun** – traditional words and melodies, arranged and recorded by A&C Black.

The following copyright holders have kindly given their permission for the inclusion of their copyright material in the book and on the audio CD:

Fossils from *Carnival of the Animals* by Saint Saëns, performed by the Scottish National Orchestra, conducted by Alexander Gibson, CD CFP 4086, © 1975 EMI Records.

Jockey's Dance from *Snow-White and the Seven Dwarfs* by Eleanor Alberga © Music Link International, 1998 for the CD, © RDF Ltd, 1994 for the music.

Maja pade words and music by Niru Desai, © 1982 Niru Desai.

March Past of the Kitchen Utensils from *The Wasps* by Vaughan Williams, performed by the London Philharmonic Orchestra, conducted by Sir Adrian Boult, CDM 764020 2, © 1987 EMI Records Ltd.

Prehistoric Animal Brigade © words and music by M L Reeve. Used by permission of the M L Reeve Estate.

Qing Feng Shou (Celebrations of good harvest - 'Chinese kitchen') from CD China/Chudia wind and percussive Ensembles. Cat Auvidis-Unesco D8209.

Sun arise by Rolf Harris and Harry Butler © 1963, EMI Records Ltd.

Sextet from *Dancing with the shadow* by Eleanor Alberga from British Women Composers – Vol 2. Cat no: LNT 103.

Every effort has been made to trace and acknowledge copyright owners. If any right has been omitted, the publishers offer their apologies and will rectify this in subsequent editions following notification. (The publishers regret that it has not been possible to trace the copyright of **Gonna build a house boat** nor the copyright of **Mi caballo blanco**, attributed to Francisco Flores del Campo.)